LIES THAT SHAPED YOU

An Unconventional Practical Guide to Help You Rewrite Your Reality, Elevate Your Life and Reclaim Your Freedom

YASMEN AHMED

ACKNOWLEDGEMENTS

With any big project or undertaking like this book, there was no way it would have been born and brought to you today without the support of my loved ones.

This book wouldn't be in your hands if it was not for the support of my soulmate, best friend, and husband Amr.

It was thanks to you that I was able to keep going with the vision for this book despite my (MANY) breakdowns while writing. Anytime I felt like I was drowning, you were there to pull me out. Thank you for being my rock, my inspiration, and my home since the moment we met.

This book also wouldn't have come into fruition without my parents who have been my guiding light on this journey to success. I owe all my growth to you and can't thank you both enough for teaching me the importance of having a big heart, being humble, making an impact and being a lifelong learner.

This book is also in your hands thanks to both my sisters who are my best friends and have held my hand during every up and down. Thank you to my big sister Hend for being my constant role model, for giving me strength and always gifting me with the exact wise words that I always need to hear.

And obviously, I would never forget (or else, she would kill me) a special thank you to my younger sister Sara for being a source of joy and laughter in my life. My life became brighter ever since you were born. Thank you for helping me see the light inside of me even when I couldn't see it myself.

I would also like to thank my beautiful grandma (my tata) for being my inspiration and all the lessons she taught me as a young girl that made me the woman I am today. She will always be in my heart and I hope I make her proud.

I also want to give a huge thanks to all the amazing souls in the @inspirewithyas community on Instagram. Your continuous support for me and my work means the world to me. This book is for you.

Last but definitely not least, I want to thank YOU, the reader. Your time is the greatest gift you can give, and I'm so grateful for it. In return, I hope this book supports and inspires you in ways you didn't even know possible.

I hope this book is the catalyst that will spring board you towards your most authentic you, the spark that ignites your truest self and helps you finally make the life of your dreams a reality.

NOTE TO YOU

"Dear society, if you cannot inspire me, do not demolish me either."

Let's start with a question. What would you go back and tell your younger self?

After nearly finishing my writing for ANOTHER book with a completely different topic, I suddenly changed direction. I found myself being called to write THIS book and talk about this topic instead. Why? Well, I asked myself very two simple questions:

If today was my last day on this earth, what would I want everyone to know?

What would I go back and tell my younger self?

The information in this book was IT.

And trust me, I went down a really deep rabbit hole learning and unlearning all that I've been told from society over the years. Heck, I'm STILL unlearning today.

That's life.

Unlearning the things that are no longer serving you.

Unlearning the things that are not aligned with your true soul purpose.

Unlearning the things holding you back from your greatest potential.

So, from my heart to yours, I do hope that one day I can connect with every single one of you who decided to read this book. What I would give to sit down with you and listen to your life stories; the good, the ugly and the hard.

But what keeps my heart happy is that I know that by reading the words in this book, we will become connected like no other through our journey of growth, unlearning and awakening. Also, I know time is one of THE most valuable and precious assets you have in this lifetime, so I just wanted to thank you for gifting me with some of yours as you read this book.

Now, a little note:

No matter who you are or where you're from, please approach the concepts in this book with an open mind and see what aligns or resonates with you.

Your truth is individual to you. No one can tell you otherwise. Your truth is yours and yours alone. Your truth does not need validation or proof. You can feel your truth in your bones and this is what I want to ask for you to become aware of.

What resonates? What hits a cord? Triggers you? Pay attention.

I simply want this book to be a source of insights, awakening and breakthroughs to encourage you to break free from the invisible cages that may be holding you back. The cages keeping you small.

My hope is that the knowledge and tips in this will help you finally step into freedom. Not perceived freedom. But real and authentic freedom that is yours.

My own journey of discovering, learning and unlearning was born when I hit an emotional, mental and physical rock bottom, which is something I would never wish upon anyone and trust me, you'll get the details of that later.

But this is why writing this book just poured out of me as soon as I decided to write it. I knew these new ways of thinking were needed for this current society with all the struggles that we are facing as a whole.

This is why I put everything I know into this book.

This book is written not only for you but for generations to come.

I feel so grateful to know that the knowledge can be accessed by anyone who feels called to make changes before hitting any sort of emotional, mental or physical rock bottom. And if rock bottom is the place you currently are at, this book is especially for you.

Even if you're feeling lost, frustrated or unfulfilled and desire to finally be the MAIN CHARACTER in your life story – the one in control, then you've definitely picked up the right book.

If you walk away from this book feeling a newfound hope, inner peace, or had a light bulb moment then…that is gold.

So, from my soul to yours, thank you for choosing this book. And most importantly, thank yourself for showing up for yourself by reading this book. I'm honored we get to spend this time together. Now, shall we begin?

PREFACE

"Society attacks early, when the individual is helpless." – B. F. Skinner

Here's the harsh truth: **You've been lied to.**

Dear you,

You have been fed a whole bunch of lies.

For much of your life, you have been told certain things that you, over time, came to believe were true. They may still be true to you. You were given labels, classifications, put in boxes, and told that you were only meant to go so far.

You may have been told that you are not strong enough, not smart enough, and even not aggressive enough. That your level of "intelligence" isn't great, and that is why you will never succeed. That your attitude will just not be accepted in the corporate world.

You may have been told that your perceived weaknesses and flaws are holding you back from learning certain subjects, accomplishing certain tasks, earning awards, or being a leader.

You may have been told that only "lucky" people get ahead in life. That you must fit in to achieve success. That you need to look a certain way, eat a certain way, or talk a certain way to be loved or desired.

You may have been told that your dreams will never come true. That you have to settle. That you will never find what you want out there.

But... you are being lied to.

These inaccuracies that have been and are continuing to be pushed by society are simply wrong. This society is still immersed in the limited mindset of the past.

But now, as more and more individuals are stepping up and sharing their stories, we are finding out that these beliefs are simply not true. That we have only been fed lies by society.

It's usually when people hit their mid-life crisis that they start to wake up and see the truth, but by then, they feel it's "too late" for them to make any changes or get out of the game.

They feel like the truth had already been snatched for them and they lived a life of lies.

Well, it is time we start paying attention and putting an end to this.

No longer should we buy into the lies about what success is, what happiness is, what defines our worth, what it means to be masculine or feminine, and so many more things that we have been fed.

For a long time, I was totally brainwashed into thinking I was fundamentally wrong just for the way I was. And I'm sure you've felt that way too. All these lies (as well as so many more) have made us believe in things that messed up our bodies, minds, and emotions. They have pushed us into buying into things that negatively impacted our physical and mental well-being.

But once you find and understand the truth, you become immune to all of those lies. You finally set yourself free. You break out of all those chains and ropes that have been holding you down, the cages and ties deeply wrapped around you. You put an end to the never-ending cycle that has been going on for what feels like forever.

It's none other than these sneaky little lies that come together in a symphony and brainwash billions of us into doing, buying, and eating things that are bad for us. We end up spending our hard-earned money on large companies who get us addicted to ingredients that destroy our health. And it's not just hurting us, but our children and the entire generations to come. The same goes for future generations. And so, the cycle continues.

The key to breaking free is to wake up and see through all the lies that we have been fed. Once we stop falling for the lies, we take away the power that these companies have. We strip them of this power that enables them to destroy our health and well-being.

So, let's put an end to this deception that's been affecting billions of us.

Share this book and let's open everyone's eyes to the truth.

Imagine if we could finally, together, leave this matrix, this rate race, and the toxic system that we're all tangled in. And be free. No longer trapped by the fake limitations we thought were holding us back. No longer limited by the labels we were given in high school.

The power of labels can be incredibly toxic when used in the wrong way. Growing up, I was given all sorts of labels like "introverted," "weak," "dumb," "chubby," and even "too girly." I also suffered with a stutter that caused me horrible anxiety. But just because some people in high school slapped those labels on me doesn't mean they are true. Or that I would be held back by them.

Now, let's take a step back and talk about how these beliefs get programmed in us in the first place.

It all starts with our development in early childhood, when our minds are like sponges. Between the ages of 0 to 7, we soak up and absorb everything around us. In essence, this is when most of our subconscious programming happens (also because we're in a theta brain wave state during these years of our lives). And if we don't actively work on changing those beliefs, they will keep running in our minds even today.

You see, back then, our little minds didn't have any existing belief systems to oppose the new information. So, we just silently kept accepting everything that we learned as truth. We simply had no previous experiences to challenge the new input with. And that's how we end up with firm beliefs from our early childhood days that stick with us for the rest of our lives.

By the age of 7, we have this firm set of beliefs that becomes progressively tough to change. All the information we have absorbed and stored throughout the years stays with us the rest of our lives – unless we make a special effort to challenge and change it.

And, as we pass that age, whenever we come across new information, our subconscious mind assesses it against our existing beliefs to see if the former fits. Then, it either accepts or rejects the new information based on that. This is why our minds are often biased and choose to only accept experiences that confirm our current belief systems and disregard the rest.

For example, if you have firm belief that "everyone I meet takes advantage of me," then you will only focus on the relationships or friendships where you feel this belief has been confirmed, instead of acknowledging the healthy connections you might already have in your life, which sadly don't receive your attention.

Let's take another belief as an example: "I will always be chosen last." When you have this belief, your attention will solely be on experiences where you have been picked last, be it during your school days, college years, or even in your professional life. These types of beliefs are what often lead to self-fulfilling prophecies, since you are already expecting it to happen.

This explains why our early experiences have the biggest impact on our happiness and level of success in life. Our beliefs become the core foundation for our perception of the world afterwards.

Now, beforehand, I was completely unaware that we even had subconscious beliefs, and that these beliefs make up **95%** of who we are today!

I only came to learn this during one of my Clinical Hypnotherapy trainings and, to say the least, I was shocked.

Frustrated. Annoyed. Cheated. (These words definitely summed it up)

How was this never taught to us before?

That's why lasting change is so damn difficult.

How are we NOT aware of where 95% of our programming and beliefs come from? That these beliefs make up 95% of who we are?

How are these beliefs (that we were so unaware of) driving our choices, behaviors, and emotions?

Everyone has a motive for doing the things that they do.

And here I am, writing this book. So, what is *my* agenda?

Well, I simply want this book to be your catalyst for freedom. The key that unlocks and reveals the truth hidden behind all the lies. My ultimate goal is to open just one person's eyes to what is really happening around us. To be conscious of the systems we've been put into and have become stuck in.

That is how I define success for me and this book – expanding your mind, helping you reach a whole new level of awareness, and ultimately giving you the freedom you so rightly deserve.

The freedom to CHOOSE what you really want in life, not what society or school or even your parents tell you to want. The freedom to live the life YOU want. Because, guess what? Your dreams were given to you for a purpose. They are meant to be pursued, to be lived out, so you can have the life you've always wanted deep down. And let me tell you, you deserve it. You are worthy of it all.

This book is aimed at widening your mind to the possibility of what is possible for you. Please use all the information you get from here and use it as tools to break free from the system, discover your own truth, and live life on your own terms.

So, are you ready to dive into the rabbit hole?

Table of Content

INTRODUCTION 20

THE REALITY 29

HOW TO READ THIS BOOK 36

WHO IS THIS BOOK FOR? 43

CHAPTER 1 47

LIE #1: YOU ARE THE VICTIM OF YOUR CIRCUMSTANCES 47

ARE YOU TRAPPED? 52

VICTIM MINDSET 53

HIDDEN PLEASURE 59

THE 6 HUMAN NEEDS 65

HOW TO BREAK FREE 73

CHAPTER 2 83

LIE #2: BURNOUT IS "NORMAL" 83

"I'M SO TIRED" 98

HOW TO BREAK FREE 105

CHAPTER 3 112

LIE #3: TRADITIONAL EDUCATION EMPOWERS YOU 112

EXTRAVERT VS INTROVERT 122

THE BIGGEST LIE 128

WHERE DID OUR CREATIVITY GO? 131

HOW TO BREAK FREE 137

CHAPTER 4 143

LIE #4: WORKING THE 9-5 IS THE ONLY WAY TO ACHIEVE SUCCESS 143

THE RAT RACE 151

HOW TO BREAK FREE 161

CHAPTER 5 169

LIE #5: TALKING ABOUT MONEY IS TABOO 169

HAPPY MONEY VS UNHAPPY MONEY 176

HOW TO BREAK FREE 180

CHAPTER 6 .... **182**

LIE #6: MONEY IS THE ROOT OF ALL EVIL 182

HOW TO BREAK FREE 193

CHAPTER 7 204

LIE #7: YOUR WORTH IS BASED ON SOMETHING EXTERNAL 204

THE MAN, THE BOY, AND THE DONKEY 217

WHAT'S THE STORY YOU TELL YOURSELF?... 222

HOW TO BREAK FREE 223

CHAPTER 8 230

LIE #8: YOUR VALUE AS A HUMAN IS BASED ON YOUR BODY SIZE 230

HOW TO BREAK FREE 241

CHAPTER 9 249

LIE #9: WHEN YOU FIND LOVE, EVERYTHING WILL BE PERFECT 249

YOU HAVE TO SETTLE 257

HOW TO BREAK FREE 259

CHAPTER 10 265

LIE #10: FEMININE ENERGY IS A WEAKNESS ...265

THE TAKEAWAY 268

HOW TO BREAK FREE 270

CHAPTER 11 279

LIE #11: YOU NEED MORE TO BE HAPPY 279

HOW TO BREAK FREE 283

FINAL THOUGHTS 289

CONNECT WITH ME 293

REFERENCES 295

INTRODUCTION
THE CAVE

You're in a cave with no light in it other than a fire. In the cave, you're one of the prisoners chained up facing a wall.

The wall is the only thing you see.

Behind you, there's a fire that casts light and shadow on the wall that's in front of you.

You don't know this nor do you see this, but there are people who walk on a raised walkway with puppets which create shadows on the wall of your cave.

So, naturally, you perceive the shadows you see on the wall as your reality.

Because that's all you know, that's all you've ever seen.

Being in this cave is your life.

Then one day, you find a way and escape the cave. You become free. Free from everything that you thought was reality.

You begin to move into the real world and you gain a greater sense of what is real.

You see the sun and find yourself speechless of its ability to give light and life to this other world.

You begin to realize that there was another life outside of the cave all along – A much more beautiful and brighter life.

You realize that what you knew before was not the truth.

Slowly, you begin to reach another level of understanding of life. After experiencing this greater reality, you're excited to return to the cave to convince the others to escape and experience this outside world with you. But when you return to the cave, your eyes can no longer see in the darkness of the cave. You're no longer able to see the shadows of the objects on the wall, which was all you knew before.

The others laugh at you as your eyes cannot adjust back to the darkness inside the cave.

And you realize that you can't stay in the cave any longer after experiencing this other new world.

You can no longer be a prisoner.

Because once you've gained this knowledge of more, going back to complete ignorance is impossible.

"The mind, once stretched by a new idea, never returns to its original dimensions." –Ralph Waldo Emerson

Hi There!

What you just read was a much MUCH simpler re-telling of the allegory by the philosopher Plato called Plato's cave.

What I love about this story is that there are so many important lessons we can learn. When I first heard this story while studying Philosophy at A level, it stuck with me. It was like truth smacked me in the face, and I couldn't get it out of my head.

The allegory digs into the idea of how humans perceive reality and if human existence has a higher truth. In simple terms, I believe the prisoner who escapes the cave represents an individual seeking knowledge. We're all trapped in some sort of "cave" keeping us imprisoned.

Are we in a cave as well? Is there some grander, more beautiful reality beyond us? Waiting for us to discover?

Whether it's our limiting beliefs, false stories, childhood experiences, or societal conditioning, it's our responsibility to find our truth and create the reality we desire on our own terms. All of the brainwashing we've received is only holding us back. And it's on us to break free.

This idea of questioning our reality and our own perceptions is a theme seen in movies such as The Matrix, The Truman Show, and books like Fahrenheit 451 by Ray Bradbury.

Think of movie The Matrix, where a group of people are shown being obedient, on auto-pilot, just going through the motions while a dark truth about their reality remains concealed and hidden.

Think of the movie The Truman Show, where the main character Truman Burbank lives in a false reality with his every move being filmed and broadcasted to millions of households, until one day he discovers that his life is all a lie.

Think of the book Fahrenheit 451, where the main character pulls away from society and its rules in order to find the "true" society.

Look how, in all these examples, the character begins in a state of ignorance then learns that they must transcend out of this state into a world of knowledge to learn the truth.

Just like Plato's "Allegory of the Cave", escaping the cave is required to grow as a person. And this book is here to help you break free from the shackles from the cave that's been holding you back. It's time to say goodbye to all those false stories you've been fed about yourself, the lies about what you can and can't do, what's possible and what's not. It's time to unlearn those limiting beliefs that were drilled into you when you were just a child.

By simply picking up this book, you're one step closer to the sweet freedom of becoming the person you're destined to be.

Writing this book was probably the hardest thing I ever did. But the book is now complete, and I'm honored to place it in your hands.

This book was so difficult to write because it required me to go into the depths and shadows of myself that I have been avoiding so that I can be completely and utterly vulnerable with you.

This is a book I needed to read myself.

And I'm so happy it's finally done.

All you need to achieve your freedom is here.

It's right here in the pages of this book. Yours for the taking.

I want this book to be a beacon of hope, a reminder that your current life can transform into the dream life you've always wanted. I mean it. It really can.

If mine did, yours definitely can too.

The Game

Many said life is meant to be a struggle.

Many said that all rich people are criminals and evil.

Many said having a university diploma is required for success.

Many said your job is everything.

Many said you can finally "enjoy your life" when you retire.

Many said entertainment and binging TV is the best way to relax.

Many said buying more things makes you happy.

Many said success is having a 9-5 corporate job.

Many said being feminine is weak.

Many said you can't have it all.

Many said making money is difficult.

Many said only lucky people get what they want.

Many said women need to be thin in order to be attractive and desired.

Many said being perfect is what you need to be to succeed.

I believed in all of this…before I knew.

So, you might be thinking, "Whoa, that was a lot to take in."

It is. I know.

But don't worry, I'm with you.

When I learnt the truths I'm sharing in this book, my reality of what I thought was "true" completely shattered. That's why I must warn you, after finishing this book, you will see the world differently.

Everything will look and feel different.

You will begin to notice things that you may have not noticed before.

You will be more aware.

More conscious.

More awake.

More in control.

And most importantly, more powerful.

You will understand how to remove limitations and blocks that have been sabotaging you this whole time. You will understand how many of these blocks are actually self-created and learn how to master your mind, body and life.

When you learn the truth, it's like finally cleaning your glasses when you didn't even know your lenses were dirty all along.

You finally see things more clearly. As they really are.

Not how they were told or taught to you.

Now, let's get one thing clear, this book isn't just some "woo-woo" stuff. Everything I talk about here is real and is sabotaging your work, relationships, finances, success, and happiness.

The lies that you've been fed through societal conditioning are controlling not only your current life but all the previous generations before you.

And you know what the best thing is? By picking up this book, you've already decided that enough is enough.

It's up to you to take responsibility to become the one who will break the societal and generational patterns.

Because, honestly, it's not your parent's responsibility, not your teacher's responsibility nor your friend's responsibility to help you become the person you know deep down you are destined to be.

Trust me, I know it's so much easier to blame society, your parents, your grandparents, the government, the media or your culture for your unhappiness or lack of success and fulfillment.

I did for a long time as I lived in blame and victim mode for the majority of my life.

But then I realized I just became like the majority by complaining, huffing and puffing and wishing my life was different… but taking NO responsibility for anything and not making any changes.

I mean, every day I was doing the exact same thing, thinking the same negative thoughts, mindlessly scrolling social media, people-pleasing and choosing to focus on the lack that surrounds me… How in the world did I expect miraculous change when I was in such a low vibrational state?

"Insanity is doing the same thing over and over expecting different results." – Rita Mae Brown, Sudden Death

I mean I didn't like being around ME. So why would abundance, love, and fulfillment come and join me when I was sending out this misery into the world around me?

But after hitting my lowest rock bottom in my mental and physical health, I had no choice but to take responsibility and wake up so I can wake others up too.

THE REALITY

It's absolutely absurd how the majority of us are feeling unfulfilled in our day to day without realizing that we are just one step away from living an EXTRAORDINARY life.

Just because it's become the norm for everyone else to settle for an average "meh" life doesn't mean you have to follow suit.

"It's lonely at the top. Ninety-nine percent of people in the world are convinced they are incapable of achieving great things, so they aim for mediocrity." – Tim Ferris

Isn't it funny how we entertain children when it comes to their big dreams, but then frown, scold, and shake our heads in dismay when adults say they want more in life and aren't happy with the status quo?

It's because the majority of people are living on auto-pilot, and that's what society deems as "normal". If you truly desire a life that is beautiful, fulfilling, exciting, filled with passion, you're immediately labeled as a "dreamer" or told to "be more realistic."

Take a look around you. The majority of people are comfortable with just settling for the average, mediocre, lowest update of their version of their lives. I've found that they'd rather stick to the same old routine than chase after something bigger and more amazing. They actually do anything to AVOID living a larger, grander, and more beautiful life. A life that is their dream life.

And that's not even their fault.

It's just the system around us that we're stuck in. It's not designed to help us thrive or empower us. It's built to keep us compliant, not encouraging us to dream big.

They want us to be workers, not thinkers.

That's why we're given rules of what's "normal" and what is expected of us.

They want us to fit into their little box.

That's why we're told that we're only capable of so much. That we have a limited level of potential and skill.

They want us to settle for a small, mundane life with a stable, steady income (even if we're unhappy or completely miserable).

That's why we're made to believe that this kind of mediocre life is the "dream" and we shouldn't ask for more.

They want us to believe that wanting more is selfish and greedy.

Have you noticed how movies and shows often portray rich people as evil and corrupt? So, of course, YOU shouldn't want money. Because money is, of course, the root of all evil. Because it will "change you and make you some sort of criminal" too.

Society then tells you to look at the people who dared to pursue their creative dreams and how they all ended up becoming starving artists, barely scraping by. So, of course, you shouldn't follow your dreams. Because it will make you "broke and desperate" too.

But guess what? Those beliefs are IMAGINARY. They are shaped by the false ideology created by society's rule of keeping us small and limited.

The truth is that you are a limitless being. You have infinite possibilities at the tips of your fingers. You can create, be, do, and be anything your heart desires.

Look at the nature that surrounds you. Do you see anything that just stays stagnant or the same? No, right? That's because nature and the universe is forever expanding and growing. If they stop moving, they simply cease to exist.

And you know what? You're just like that too. You also have this immense potential within you that knows no bounds. So, shouldn't it be your natural purpose in life to reach your potential and keep growing as well?

Nature never says still. And neither should you.

Now this idea of you being limitless might sound familiar to you. Why?

Because, deep down, your soul has always known the truth. It knew all along how powerful and limitless you are. You knew it as a child before society got its hands on your mind and knocked the truth out.

Your true self has been patiently waiting for you to wake up.

And now, the steps highlighted in this book will help you wake up, shake off those limiting beliefs, unlearn false stories about yourself, and tap back into your infinite realm of possibility.

This book will equip you with what you need in order to become the person you've always wanted to be. To become the dream person your younger self believed they could be.

The knowledge in this book will set you up for the rest of your life.

If you let it.

Before you continue, I want to remind you that we can only strive to become better, NOT perfect.

Life is all about course-correcting, adapting, and growing.

You aren't given this one life to just simply survive. It's your duty to live a life where you thrive. A life that fills your heart with joy. And not only for yourself, but also for those who hold dear.

Think of it like this: Each one of us is all tied up tightly with ropes, keeping every body part in place, keeping us stuck. These ropes hold us back from reaching our full potential and living our best lives.

The ropes are like baggage that we've picked up along the way. Each rope is created through negative past experiences, traumas, fears, failures, insecurities, self-limiting beliefs, and rules that we "should follow".

But here's the kicker: The strongest ropes holding us back are the invisible ones. We don't see them. We don't even know they are there. They are like invisible puppet strings that control us without us even knowing it.

These invisible ropes are usually the conditioning we've received from society and the collective lies that we've been programmed with – which this book will dive into.

This book will help you get a pair of scissors to cut through all these ropes and finally break free.

It's time to prioritize yourself, level up your life, and become the best version of you possible.

This book is not your typical self-help nonsense.

It will give you the tools you need to achieve freedom in all areas of your life.

No more being stuck in the rat race. It's time to craft your own happiness and success. It's time to help yourself so that you an help others too.

With this book, you'll be the one calling the shots. It will give you the freedom to live life on your own terms, not someone else's.

This book gives you the building blocks to where this freedom resides, no matter what your past circumstances or mistakes may be. It's about time you broke free from the system or the "rat race". Despite how deep you think you are in it, let me tell you…

There is ALWAYS a way out.

You'll see.

This is especially true in this time we live in, where a universe of knowledge is just a tap away on the small device that's always in our hands.

A time where you can build a million-dollar business online right from the comfort of your cozy home, while you wear your PJs.

A time where YouTubers, gamers, or TikTokers are making 7 figures.

A time where you can connect with people from all around the world in an INSTANT through social media or video calls.

A time where what was previously deemed "impossible" has become part of our normal day to day.

I mean, we are talking about creating a whole civilization ON MARS. If that doesn't sound too "crazy" of a goal, how is you changing your life into a life that is beyond your wildest dreams crazy?

This book will help you make the choices you want to make, rather than blindly obeying and following what the market or society tries to shove down your throat. Forget those multibillion-dollar advertising industries that continuously tell you what to eat, when to eat, what to buy, what's trending, what's attractive, or how you should look. Don't let them think they can control your every move anymore.

It's finally your time to break free and live life on your own terms.

HOW TO READ THIS BOOK

In this book, I'm bringing together my knowledge from studying Psychology in university and my professional training as a therapist in Cognitive Behavioral Therapy, Psychotherapy, and Counseling. I'm also a Clinical Hypnotherapist, Thetahealer (a practitioner in energy healing), and NLP (Neuro-Linguistic Programming). I combine the wisdom from these modalities as well as my own life experiences and extensive work with clients to create simple and practical principles that I know will support and help you in breaking free from the imaginary boundaries you've placed on yourself.

These principles in this book will also help you heal and form an entire new reality of your life. A life where you can exercise freedom in all areas. A life where you can create the emotional, physical, and financial reality you desire. A life where you can just be authentically you. Free from society's expectations and rules and so much more.

So, take your time. Take it one page at a time. One sentence at a time. Dive into all the ideas presented in this book and let them soak in. Imagine all the possibilities that are open to you, waiting for you.

While reading this book, think about what ideas make you question things and spark your curiosity. More importantly, pay attention to what feels like the truth for you deep in your heart and soul. Pay attention to what creates an expansive feeling in you, but also triggers you. Noticing your triggers is important as they are messengers pointing you toward what might need acknowledging and healing.

You don't have to read this whole book.

Nor do you have to read from the first page until the very last.

You can read whatever catches your interest or any of the topics that pull you in.

Unless you feel guided to do otherwise.

When I ask people why they don't like reading books, they say it's because they usually get bored in the middle chapters. And I get it – it's completely normal. As someone who has loved reading pretty much my entire life and found safety and comfort in books,

I can positively say that I also sometimes feel bored reading certain books.

But here's the thing: if you're feeling that boredom, it might mean that those chapters just aren't resonating with you. And that's OK! You don't have to force yourself to trudge through them. Instead, please feel guided to read the chapters that resonate with you the most. The ones that really pique your interest and curiosity.

You have my full permission to do so because I believe anyone and everyone can benefit from this book, and I want you to have full control over how you want to read this book. In a way that suits you best.

You can skip a few pages ahead, jump to a different chapter, or even start reading in the middle until the end. Don't hesitate to flip around and read only the specific chapters that speak to you the most. If you feel called out to see only those parts, simply read them only.

Why does this idea of not reading from start to finish make us feel discomfort?

Well, I believe it's due to the traditional teaching methods in schools that taught us that when we start at the beginning of something, we must follow it right to the end, or we are a failure somehow. It's this pressure, in my opinion, why many of us don't like reading.

We feel pressured to remember and learn every single word that the book says and continue pushing ourselves to read it, even when we no longer want to.

And I don't want you to do that when you're reading or listening to this book. Forget about all that noise. Let go of any expectations, assumptions, or pressure to read it chronologically or in a specific way.

Who knows, maybe just one sentence in this whole book will turn out to be all that you needed to make the changes necessary.

You can pick up this book, read a few chapters, pick up another book, and then come back to this book whenever you feel called to do so.

As an avid reader, I've done this many times and let me tell you – it's one of the best ways to absorb knowledge without getting "bored" of reading the same book for a while. This is something I've learned from my husband, who also loves reading.

We all crave variety, even when it comes to books with their stories and narrative tones.

HOW THIS BOOK IS SPLIT UP

This book is split into chapters each covering ONE specific topic and a societal "lie" that has been programmed into us – the culprit of what's holding us back.

Each chapter then simply ends with some practical bullet points to help you break free from this lie and regain your freedom.

Now, if you find yourself gaining some insight and inspiration, feeling less alone, or having an "aha" moment while reading this book, it's safe to say that I have done my job.

And can I be honest?

I have huge respect for you choosing to read this book. For choosing to improve, grow, challenge, and change your life for the better. Because, honestly, most people don't.

Most people prefer to stay in the small, the comfortable, and the familiar. But not you.

We both know you're not most people.

That's why you're here.

It's a pleasure to meet you.

WARNING: Before we go any further, I just want to make sure that you're ready to continue.

Because once you dive into this book, there's no going back.

What you will learn here, you can never unlearn.

Just like that scene in The Matrix movie when Neo made the choice to take the red pill. Your life will be changed forever.

Trust me, it's easier to ignore the signs, stay passive, and continue living within the seemingly cozy bubble society has built for us.

There, it feels safe.

But as it may be safe, it keeps you small, caged, and constricted.

Is that really what life should be about?

The way society has been fundamentally created actually crushes our spirits and potential.

This book uncovers the ways we've been cheated through the schooling system, the "corporate" trap, the ridiculous pressure to "keep up with the Joneses", the toxic beliefs we're fed about money, lies about our self-image, self-worth, fad diets, and so much more.

This book will uncover how we, as individuals, have been misled toward living unfulfilled lives, constantly chasing the next "new thing", comparing ourselves to everyone else, and making bad decisions along the way.

I'm here to tell you that ignorance is NOT bliss.

But how can you escape a cage you didn't even know you were trapped in?

Well, my friend, you chose and picked up (or downloaded, heck, it's the 21st century) THIS book for a reason. A reason that could be so much bigger than you ever thought to believe.

This book will allow you to wake up from the hypnotic slumber you've been put under, thanks to societal conditioning.

I mean, why is it that when a baby is born, they call it a miracle; but as we grow older, we are just expected to settle for the mediocre?

You shouldn't be OK with just being mediocre.

You should aim for something more. For fulfillment. Excitement. Happiness. Peace.

"The big win is when you refuse to settle for average or mediocre," – Seth Godin

And hey, one QUICK thing: if you don't make courageous choices for yourself, no one else will.

This book will help you see that there is not only one path to freedom, but limitless pathways.

Yet every path starts with the same moment. **The bold moment when you decide to choose yourself.**

The purpose of this book is to help you break free from the mental and societal cages, the matrix, and the limiting system in order to be the driver of your own life and take control back.

And hey, feel free to join the inspired Instagram community on @inspirewithyas to always feel supported, seen, and heard. Also let me know if you're reading the book too!

WHO IS THIS BOOK FOR?

This book is for the person who has dreams that others might not understand.

The person who wants to be an independent thinker.

The person who is searching for more out of life.

The person who no longer wants to be a victim to society's choices.

The person who has tried the "traditional" way but it hasn't worked out.

The person who wants to finally feel understood and empowered.

The person who has dreams that others might not understand.

The person who is fed up with playing by the other people's rules.

The person who is unfulfilled and wants to reclaim their life back.

The person who wants to feel free and happy in all areas of their life.

The person who feels like their life isn't complete and is searching for that last missing puzzle piece to finally experience happiness, success, and freedom.

If any of the above resonated with you, then maybe this book is the very thing you need.

It's time to start thinking for yourself. Don't let society think for you any longer.

This leads us to the big question…

Are you ready for breakthroughs?

Because let me tell you, there's a whole lot more to our reality than what you've been told and taught.

This book can change your life, but only IF you're willing to let it. If you're open to the possibilities.

It will help you break free from that limited mold that society created to keep you small.

This book can be your ultimate guide to finding true freedom, no matter what your past looks like and no matter how far deep you think you are in the system.

Remember – there is ALWAYS a way out.

Plus, as a BONUS, while reading this book, you can access my "secret proven success formula to making your goals a reality (in under 1 year" for FREE by visiting my website: https://www.inspirewithyas.com/goalsettingebook

This book is not your typical self-help nonsense. It's a book that will help you **thrive** and no longer simply just survive. And most importantly, not settle into a life that you don't desire.

Disclaimer: Whenever the word "they" is mentioned throughout this book, think of it as the system that society operates from. It is

not aimed at one person, one government, or culture. It's about the whole system we are born into and are currently living in.

And hey, I may be the author of this book who's holding a brighter lamp with this knowledge, but I'm still wandering through the dark caves right alongside you while I continually grow, unlearn, and relearn too.

Now, it's time to take things to the next level.

Get ready to dive in together.

It's time to seriously question the way things have been done in the past, to rewrite YOUR OWN RULES and do life and business YOUR way.

Are. You. Ready?

CHAPTER 1

LIE #1: YOU ARE THE VICTIM OF YOUR CIRCUMSTANCES

"How dare you settle for anything less when the world has made it so easy for you to be remarkable?" – Seth Godin

We are born free.

But as the years go by, we become caged.

As we grow older, we give up our power and let society do all the thinking for us.

What if I told you that it's not you that is broken but the system around us?

What if I told you that the system (society) itself was built this way?

I mean, we are meant to be independent and creative thinkers, living fulfilled lives that bring us joy. But most of us? We're not. The majority of us settle for small, boring lives, never even realizing our true potential. We settle into the mediocre "meh" life, thinking it's the only option.

I mean, everyone else is doing it, right?

Isn't that what's *normal*?

Most people just live their lives on auto-pilot, constantly chasing after the next big thing that they've been told will bring them happiness, a promotion, a new bag, a slimmer body, or a cure for loneliness.

But here's the thing: many of us are totally oblivious to the fact that our perception of reality is actually shaped by beliefs that were programmed unconsciously into us growing up.

These beliefs are ingrained in us from all sorts of places – our parents, our upbringing, generational beliefs, traditional education system (which seems more interested in creating workers than independent thinkers), the corporate industry, and even the movies and TV shows we watched growing up. And let's not forget about the beauty industry, that loves to mess with our heads and make us doubt ourselves and our sense of self-worth.

Society has this whole narrative designed to keep us feeling powerless, constantly seeking validation from others and buying more stuff to trick ourselves into feeling happy and "successful".

Now, society may never stop feeding us these false narratives. But that doesn't mean we have to listen to them.

The systems we're surrounded by love making us believe that we have zero control over our own lives. But guess what? That's another lie. The way society tries to make us think that it's "normal" to settle for a life that leaves us unfulfilled is not right. And you know what's even crazier? This narrative is pretty much the same in most cultures too.

How do I know this? Well, I was born in Egypt, but when I was just a little 5-month-old baby (hey there, baby Yas), my family moved us to the UK, where I grew up and studied up until graduating university.

And then we moved again, this time to Dubai, UAE where I'm currently residing.

Being ethnically from one culture and raised in a completely different one gave me exclusive insight into two totally different worlds. I got to see things from two different perspectives, with different ways of thinking and mindsets.

Growing up, every summer, my parents would take me and my two sisters, Sara and Hend, back to Egypt for six weeks. At the time, I didn't fully understand why they wanted to keep our family, language, and cultural ties strong and alive, but now I really appreciate it (thanks mum and dad!).

So, as an introvert from a very young age, I always loved staying quiet, sitting in the corner, and observing human behavior (oh gosh, reading that back makes me sound super creepy).

But this interest in human behavior was definitely one of the reasons why I studied Psychology.

As I grew older, I realized that in both cultures, **being unhappy was just so normal.**

It was so **normal** to constantly complain about how miserable you are.

It was so **normal** to settle for dull, uninspiring, or boring marriages and relationships.

It was so **normal** to blame others (everyone) for your problems.

It was so **normal** to be dissatisfied with aspects of your life but never taking responsibility or doing anything to change them.

I also realized the significance and connection people would receive in sharing their problems with others (who also had problems) was really remarkable to me. It fascinated me how people would bond over their miseries and problems, and even compete to see who had the biggest or worst problem of them all.

I mean, the saying is true; misery does love company. And so does mediocrity.

So, let's be honest here. When we find ourselves stuck in this endless cycle of misery and always complaining about how miserable we are… how can we expect to attract the life of our dreams?

Whether it's your dream relationship, dream job, dream body, or the financial abundance you desire. If you're operating from a 3/10, how can you expect to attract 10/10 people and opportunities in your life?

We need to shift our mindset.

As Bob Proctor once said in a Facebook post of his:

"Remember, money goes where it's invited, and stays where it's welcome."

The same goes for love, inspiration, and creativity.

This book is here to help you break free from your self-imposed misery and create a life that is truly fulfilling, beautiful, and full of possibilities. Because guess what? You deserve it.

ARE YOU TRAPPED?

You know, I've found that one of the biggest things keeping us trapped in this self-imposed misery is the **victim mentality** that we often fall into. This victim mindset is what negatively impacts our day-to-day life and choices.

That's why I made this topic the very first chapter of this book because mindset is EVERYTHING. It influences how you deal with the world and with yourself, and everything in between.

Now, ask yourself some important questions to see if you're trapped in victim mindset:

- When things go south, is your automatic response to blame the world and everything else?

- When you're feeling down, do you avoid taking any responsibility for changing your views?

- Have you ever said any of these statements?

    - "The world is filled with pain and suffering, and that's that."

    - "I'm just not as lucky as everyone else."

    - "Life is just unfair."

- "It's never my fault."

If you find yourself nodding or saying yes to any of these, well, hate to break it to you, but you've got a major case of victim mindset!

But hey, no need to worry! Most of us have been there at some point. I mean, I was the QUEEN of the victim mindset dynasty (is that even a thing?) and held onto my victimhood for way too long.

So, here's the good news: If I managed to break free from it, so can you.

I'll be sharing exactly how I, along with many others, escaped the victim mindset and found true freedom.

VICTIM MINDSET

BUT FIRST… WHAT IS VICTIM MINDSET

"Experience is not what happens to a man. It is what a man does with what happens to him," – Aldous Huxley

When you have a victim mindset, you feel like life keeps happening TO you and there's simply nothing you can do about it. Because you're just a victim of your circumstances.

But this is a deadly trap.

The thing is, being in this mindset lets you off the hook for any responsibility in your life.

Why? Because it's so much easier to point fingers and blame the economy, the government, the weather, your parents, your hometown, or your education for your unhappiness or lack of success.

Blaming everyone can provide you with a short-term sense of comfort, making you believe that you're just a helpless victim of life.

That's it.

Poor you.

I will admit, playing the victim card was deeply ingrained in me. It was like second nature to me. Let me give you a few examples how:

- I blamed being the middle child for never being "seen" and always being invisible at work. I let that hold me back for years, missing out on countless opportunities and limiting my potential for growth.

- I blamed having "my mum's Egyptian genes" for being on a bit chubbier and rounder side as a child, compared to other girls in my class. So, that's WHY I always struggled with my weight as an adult. It couldn't possibly be because I devoured boxes of chocolate and pots of Ben and Jerry's cookie dough ice cream in one sitting! I mean, come on, it was obviously my "mum's Egyptian genes". (Ha, how does that even make sense?!)

- I would blame the stuttering I had as a child for my lack of confidence in networking situations, which led me to avoid social events altogether.

- I would blame my baby face for not getting any job offers.

- I would blame my manager for not giving me a raise.

- I would blame the economy for not getting any clients.

- I would blame the miserable UK weather for my low mood and lack of motivation. Clearly, it's not my fault at all. It's just the good old mother nature that's the problem.

Trust me, I could go on and on with more examples. There's SO much more. But you get the idea. This was just a little taste of the victim beliefs that kept me stuck for years.

After reading mine, you might even spot a few of your own beliefs that stopped you from going after the life you truly wanted.

A few years ago, I remember overhearing a conversation while sitting on a bus between a mother and her daughter. The daughter had just graduated university that morning, still in her graduation gown, hat, and dress.

Allow me to give you a summary of the conversation that took place between this enthusiastic, full-of-energy new graduate and her mother.

Mother: "Enjoy today because tomorrow, the real pain and suffering of adulthood will hit you hard. Being an adult means putting up with a horrible job and boss you hate, all to pay your overdue bills. And you just got to stick it through. That's life."

After seeing her daughter's face fall, the mother quickly followed up with, "But don't worry, you'll still have your weekends to enjoy, sweetheart."

Daughter: *silence*

Mother: "Look, that's just the way things are. That's life. Happiness isn't a luxury that we have. You just have to accept it."

The daughter stayed silent, her gaze fixed on the droplets of rain racing down the bus window.

In that moment, it hit me: this girl represented hopelessness in its beginning at its rawest form. Just a few minutes ago, she was so full of joy, enthusiasm, and excitement. But her mother had just shattered her world with her own warped version of reality, the "truth" which was filled with negative beliefs, limitations, and a downright gloomy outlook.

That bus ride conversation will always stick with me, as I sat there, shaking my head. It really hurt my heart hearing what this mother was saying. I wasn't angry but sad. Sad for this woman and how she saw the world. I couldn't even imagine what kind of struggles she had faced with this mindset, and now she was passing it on to her daughter who was about to step into the adult world.

Can you imagine how difficult that girl's life will be if she adopts her mother's mindset and beliefs that life is hard, unfair, and that she has zero control over it?

That's why it's crucial for us to recognize our own limiting beliefs, and acknowledge how society plays a part in shaping them. We have to break this cycle of scarcity and negative mindset, so that we don't pass it on to the next generation.

This story of the mother and her daughter is what it's like to have a victim mindset and the challenges it can create in your lives.

You see, when you play the victim, you can conveniently blame others for all your problems, unhappiness, and the general quality of your life.

But all that blaming keeps you stuck in the past, unable to move on.

So, why do we still cling to this victim mindset, even though we know deep down it's affecting us?

Well, turns out, our unhelpful and toxic patterns and habits actually provide us a hidden pleasure.

Hidden pleasures are the sneaky benefits that you get when you do something, think a certain way, or believe in something.

For example, when you put off doing something important, you might feel a relief from stress or responsibility. These hidden pleasures are buried deep in our minds and can sway our actions and choices without us even noticing.

HIDDEN PLEASURE

The Hidden Pleasure That Victim Mindset Gives

"Many people die at 25 but aren't buried until 75," – Benjamin Franklin

- No need to take any responsibility.

- It's the easy option as it's comfortable.

- No need to put in any effort or work to make things better.

- Justifies a mediocre life which becomes acceptable.

- Gets you extra attention from others, especially family.

- Permits you to be angry and pessimistic all the time.

- Makes you feel important as others pity you.

- Connects you with others who also have problems and miseries.

- Gives you a peace of mind, knowing that you've "done your best" but "that's just life."

- Fulfills your needs for connection and community (more about this later) as it connects you with others who also have problems and miseries.

- No pressure to evolve, grow, and change your circumstances.

I know it sounds weird that I called these above points pleasure…but they are.

The following excerpt from the book Rich Dad Poor Dad by Robert Kiyosaki sums this up perfectly:

"You'd best change your point of view. Stop blaming me and thinking I'm the problem. If you think I'm the problem, then you have to change me. If you realize you're the problem, then you can change yourself, learn something, and grow wiser. Most people want everyone else in the world to change but themselves. Let me tell you, it's easier to change yourself than everyone else."

Even though most people aren't happy with the way things are, only a handful are brave enough to make a change. Because that requires taking full responsibility for your current state and quality of life, and well, that's just scary.

Taking responsibility for our lives requires us to do some serious self-reflection – to take a hard look in the mirror, our decisions, and our mindset.

It means giving up playing the victim card and owning up to our actions.

I've had many people come up to me and say, "Well, you don't understand the struggles, the traumas, and the challenges I've faced. It's not fair, and I can't just ignore what's happened."

Now, if this is you, from my heart to yours, I am deeply sorry for what you have gone through. I can't even begin to imagine the pain and suffering you have endured. Whatever happened to you in the past or during your childhood, it's definitely not your fault.

I'm not telling you to ignore what happened to you.

What I am saying is, **don't let the past define you.**

Life can be unfair sometimes, and it seriously breaks my heart to see so many children having to deal with these so-called "adults" who exploit, neglect, hurt, and traumatize them emotionally, sexually, or physically.

Even if your own childhood wasn't like that, trauma is any time you felt unsafe, ignored, neglected, or scared.

So, whatever previously happened is NOT your fault. It was never your fault. That's why it's so important to give your inner child some of that sweet, all-encompassing love, forgiveness, and compassion it has been desperately craving all these years.

But listen, can I be honest with you?

As much as it sucks what has happened to you in the past, healing and moving forward from it is on you now. **It's your responsibility to take charge and make things better starting today.**

How do you do this?

You have to take a look at your parents or the people who raised you.

How did they handle challenges?

Because a big chunk of what we know comes from what we've seen them do.

Think back to how your parents or guardians reacted when things went wrong.

Did they step up to take responsibility, take different actions, and try to make things right?

Or did they point fingers at other family members, the weather, their boss, or the government for every little mishap?

This is really important because from the age of 0 to 7, we are complete sponges, soaking up everything. And most of what we soak up is from our own parents and guardians.

So, all that we unconsciously absorb during those years can heavily shape our perception of reality, our behaviors, and our core beliefs for the rest of our lives.

It's not just the things our parents told us that shaped who we are today. It's also how they ACTED, especially when they were emotionally triggered, upset, or angry.

We learn a lot by watching and imitating others, and our parents are some of the first people we observed in this world. This is called modeling (observing and copying behaviors), and it is one of the first ways we learn to behave and act.

So, let's say your parents or guardians always played the blame game. They constantly pointed fingers at others. Or maybe they were always talking about how unlucky they were.

Maybe they had a belief that the world was completely unfair, and whenever something went wrong, they'd put the blame on everyone else instead of taking responsibility. Those beliefs might have seeped into your subconscious and have been affecting you all along.

When things don't go your way, it's much easier to blame everyone under the sun and hide at home with a tub of Ben and Jerry's ice cream, drowning in self-pity. I get it, that ice cream is tempting and all, but here's the thing: that's not the way to move forward.

Don't get me wrong, this DOES NOT mean that you can't give yourself time to grieve when things don't go according to plan. We're human, and feeling all the feels without judging yourself is part of the deal. It's totally OK in the **SHORT TERM to give yourself time to grieve and feel sorry for yourself**.

But remember to not stay there. Don't unpack your bags and settle in that pit of despair. I repeat, do NOT stay in that hollow and dark place of self-pity. Because let me tell you, it's a slippery slope. You may end up spiraling down even further.

THE 6 HUMAN NEEDS

Have you ever asked yourself why you do the things that you do?

Why does anyone do what they do?

According to Tony Robbins, a life coach and motivational speaker, there's always a reason behind our actions, and most of us are not consciously aware of it.

I mean, sometimes we do things that are absolutely illogical and ridiculous, don't we? But you know what? There are six driving forces behind all of those actions, good or bad. And those are what Tony refers to as the 6 Human Needs.

These needs are at the core of every single one of us, and they shape the way we live our lives. Even if you have a different nationality, a different skin color, different beliefs and dreams, we all have these same needs.

So, if you want to really understand why you do things and why you are the way that you are, all you have to do is learn and understand these needs, find out why you behave and react the way you do, consciously or unconsciously. This awareness can help you make real changes in your life and grow out of your victim mindset.

What are these six human needs?

1. *Certainty* – we all want a life that is stable and predictable because it's in our nature to survive.
2. *Variety* – the desire to have excitement and adventures in our lives.
3. *Significance* – feeling important and valued by others and ourselves.
4. *Love and Connection* – having meaningful relationships and emotional bonds.
5. *Growth* – self-improvement and getting better every day.
6. *Contribution* – giving back and helping others.

Now, how do these human needs get all tangled up with a victim mindset?

People with a victim mindset find comfort in the belief that they are powerless, that there's nothing they can do to change their lives, that no matter what they do, bad things are just "inevitably" going to happen to them.

This belief gives them the illusion of *certainty*, of having control over their circumstances even if it's in a negative way. They get this strange satisfaction knowing what to expect in their victimhood. It's a way of feeling secure in your helplessness.

Having a victim mindset can also make you feel special and significant. You might believe that your struggles are unique and, even if they're not, they are deserving of attention and importance. It satisfies your need for recognition and *significance* because when others give you attention and sympathy, it makes you feel special and reinforces your victim mindset.

Some people even use their victim mindset to connect with others emotionally. It's the concept of shared suffering which brings a sense of unity and belonging. The empathy and support from other people give you a twisted form of love and connection.

It reminds you that you're not alone in your suffering which also creates a sense of community, something that we all crave. And when you keep sharing your victim narrative and receiving support, it can give you a false sense of purpose and *contribution* to others who identify with the victim mindset.

The thing is, victim mindset is neither healthy nor sustainable, yet it still satisfies some of our basic human needs. Sometimes in very destructive ways. Which is why it's hard to let go and break free from this mindset.

You have to begin by recognizing these patterns and consciously redirecting these needs to healthier and more positive paths.

When life throws challenges your way, it's easy for your emotions to hijack your brain and convince you that the whole world is out to get you. That the world is "evil" and that you have no power over anything. Most of us have been there. I've certainly been in the depths of it.

But I've come to learn that we actually have a lot of control over our lives, no matter what chaos is happening around us. We CAN control a lot of things despite our external circumstances. The only thing holding us back is our own mindset.

Our minds are always searching for reasons (or should I say, excuses) to explain why we're not feeling fulfilled and happy. And the easiest thing to do is blame something or someone else, right?

But living life on autopilot is not going to bring you true success, wealth, or happiness.

I mean, you've been gifted with conscious thought for a reason.

So, get curious.

Ask.

Reflect.

Understand.

Learn.

Be better.

And help others become better.

STATEMENT OF FACT:

If you are constantly playing the victim card, you can forget about being in control of your own life. It's impossible. That's the quickest way to losing all your power.

Now, you have two choices: either you believe that life is happening to you, or you believe that life is happening FOR you. You can't have it both ways, so pick a side: are you a victim or the creator of your life?

"Your complaints, your drama, your victim mindset, your whining, your blaming, and all of your excuses have never gotten you even a single step closer to your goals or dreams. Let go of your nonsense. Let go of the delusion that you deserve better and go earn it," – Dr Steve

The rat race that we find ourselves trapped in is determined to tighten its grip on us, to keep and push us deeper in a helpless victim mentality. It wants to drain us of our most precious assets: our time, our effect, and our energy.

They know that these assets are no joke! They hold immense value. The system wants you to fall into its trap and waste your time, effort, and energy on chasing the job titles, latest cars, anger, frustration, and hopelessness. When we could use our assets instead to fuel personal growth, empowerment, and getting things done.

Having a victim mindset is like pouring fuel on the fire of jealousy and constant comparison, especially on social media. It becomes a habit in your daily life and let me tell you, it's a one-way ticket to feeling terrible.

The rat race wants to keep you trapped in that victim mindset, so you just give up on ever having a better life. And when you give up, well, that's when dangerous **hopelessness** swoops in and takes over.

Many studies have shown a strong link between hopelessness and depression. One recent study (Chen & Li, 2023) even showed how being impulsive, hopeless, depressed, and suicidal are all connected in a way.

So, by keeping us feeling hopeless and powerless, we become more susceptible to relying on any forms of distraction we can find to numb ourselves from our true feelings.

HOW DO THEY KEEP US DISTRACTED?

The rat race, in our daily grind, makes us count down and eagerly wait for the weekend, so we can finally "live" and erase the memory of our miserable weekdays.

The rat race has us seeking solace in alcohol, drugs, or binge-watching the latest Netflix series, anything to numb ourselves from the bleak and miserable reality.

It's a widespread phenomenon – the average person is unhappy with their life.

But is that any way to truly live?

This also begs the questions:

Why have we normalized misery?

Why have we come to accept and settle for mediocrity as a standard way of life?

Well, fear not! Below are the exact steps that will show you how to break free from the victim mindset and discover a newfound freedom like never before.

In the grand scheme, every twist and turn is happening for our benefit. It's happening with our growth in mind.

As life keeps moving forward, its true meaning often reveals itself only when we look back. Think back to breakups or job opportunities that you were rejected from. Didn't they lead you toward a better place today?

It's a paradox – what we think we want isn't always what we truly need.

HOW TO BREAK FREE

1. Reach Breaking Point

   This might sound a little contradictory, but just here me out.

   There comes a time, usually after a specific event, when you realize that you just CANNOT live in your current state anymore. This is when the pain of staying where you are becomes unbearable, and you realize that you need to break out of your comfort zone and make changes.

   My husband and I were listening to Tony Robbins, a motivational speaker and author, and he talks about this on his 30-day program called Personal Power (my husband was the one who got me into Tony Robbins in the first place).

   In the program, Tony says that in life, we're driven by two things: pain or pleasure.

   So, it's either inspiration or desperation that gets people to take action.

   It's often when we hit our lowest points that we really start making some serious changes that can turn our lives upside down. For me, one of my most life-changing periods was when I hit rock bottom. That's when I finally realized that I had to step up, take full responsibility, and make some serious changes.

Believe it or not, there are plenty of others who have gone through the same thing. Take Tony Robbins, for example. He used to be overweight and drowning in debt, but then he completely turned his life around. Even Hal Elrod, the bestselling author of Miracle Morning, was in $425,000 of debt, completely out of shape, and emotionally and mentally in the dumps. Can you believe he was even contemplating suicide? But he pulled himself together and now he's a massive success.

When you read life-changing, inspirational, or self-help books, you'll start noticing the same pattern. Most, if not all, success stories stem from people hitting rock bottom and being forced to take charge of their lives.

So, no matter where you are in life right now, whether you're feeling desperate or not, you have the power to make those necessary changes and break free from your mental cage.

Maybe you want to start a side hustle, run that marathon, start the gym, start a business, write that book you've been dreaming of, master a new skill, read more, get promoted in the job you love, become a millionaire, or just live your wildest dreams. I promise it's all possible.

So, where should you begin?

Well, here are two exercises that might just push you to the point of desperation needed to make REAL changes in your life.

Equipment required:

- Your beautiful self
- A pen and paper

That's it!

Step 1/2: Associate Pain With Your Current Lifestyle, Habits, or Behaviors.

Exercise #1: Write down what your life will be like if you continue living and behaving with your present mindset.

In other words, if you continue living and behaving in the same way that you are now, what will happen? How will you feel if absolutely nothing changes in your life?

Take a peek into the future, say 5, 10, or even 20 years down the road. Can you see yourself stuck in the same spot, doing the same old thing? Picture it.

What does your life look like? Where will you be? What would you have missed out on? Will your professional situation remain unchanged?

What about your personal relationships?

Will you be unhappy? Unfulfilled? Miserable? Overweight?

Sinking in regret?

Drowning in debt?

Old and bitter?

Take a moment to reflect on these questions, and spill your thoughts onto paper.

When you tie enough PAIN to a certain way of being, you eventually reach a breaking point where you simply can no longer tolerate to continue living like that. It's at this point that you finally make up your mind toward real change.

Side note: please make sure you do complete step 1 before moving on to step 2. It's a must-do, no ifs or buts. Don't fool yourself into thinking you'll get around to it later, because we both know you won't. It's now or never. I mean, you picked up this book for a reason, right?

Step 2/2: Next, Tie in the Pleasure.

Once you realize how much pain comes with your current way of doing things, the only way to not allow this to be your future is to associate pleasure with the life you can have if you make the changes necessary.

Honestly, most of us have a pretty good idea of what we need to do to improve ourselves in all areas of life. Maybe not every single little detail, but we have a rough idea, right?

Exercise #2: Journal these questions next:

- If you make changes, what do you think your life will look like?

- How will it feel to be with someone who truly loves and appreciates you?

- How will it feel to live in your dream home with your loved ones?

- How will it feel to finally give your family the life they always dreamed of?

- Think about all the places you've always dreamt of visiting; how will it feel to actually go there?

- How will it feel to no longer worry about what others think?

- How will it feel to no longer worry about the next bill or purchase?

- How will it feel to build that business you've always wanted?

- How will it feel to be confident in your own body, without any insecurities?

- How will it feel to be financially free?

Please allow your mind and body to feel all those good feelings and truly believe that everything you've written down can become a reality. Your reality.

Use these questions to break free from any limitations that others might have imposed on you and embrace these exciting new thoughts of your future. Let them become your new reality.

2. Focus on What You Can Control.

"Life will test you just before it will bless you," – Vex King; Good Vibes, Good Life

When you find yourself stuck in a situation where you feel helpless and powerless, just shift your attention to the things that you can change or have control over. This will help you regain a sense of power. Because, let's face it, you won't always be feeling on top of the world and not everything will go your way. And that's perfectly fine.

I believe that this "positive vibes only" movement has taken a wrong turn and ended up being toxic. It's this toxic positivity that dismisses the genuine, real human experience of roller coaster emotions that we're meant to feel.

It's totally OK to sometimes get sad, upset, frustrated, or angry but it's what you do after that counts. That's the crucial distinction. You can either do nothing and blame everyone (victim mindset), or you can embrace your feelings, make a plan to take action, and focus on what you can actually control in the situation.

3. **Adopt a Growth Mindset.**

   Having a victim mindset can make you think that the whole world is constantly out to get you and make your life miserable.

   But life isn't actually against you.

   It's just that the more you believe in a certain perspective, the more you attract situations that confirm your biased thinking.

   After all, the mind always wants to be "right" and will search for experiences to confirm its bias.

   Adopting a growth mindset can totally change things for you. It helps you see how the world is actually working in your favor, guiding you toward exactly what you need.

   So, what exactly is a growth mindset?

   Well, it's when:

   - You start seeing obstacles as opportunities and lessons.

   - You believe that your skills and potential are limitless and endlessly expansive.

- You ditch that narrow-minded view and start seeing things from a broader perspective.

It's all about changing your mindset and looking at things from a different angle.

Life can be pretty good to you if you let it! I highly recommend the book Mindset by Carol Dweck to dive deeper into this topic.

So yes, there are many things in life that you can't control, many experiences that are so painful (trust me, I know), but it's up to you how you handle it. It's your sole responsibility to decide how you're going to react or respond to whatever life throws at you.

So, when you hit those tough times, try seeing them as opportunities for growth or a shield protecting you from something else. All the hardships, the bumps, the challenges down the road are helping you *grow*.

I know it's not easy to think in this way, but the more you do it, the easier it gets.

The mind is just like a muscle you work out.

And before you know it, you will start noticing that life's just pushing you to level up. It's showing you that what went down was a blessing in disguise, maybe a way of keeping you safe somehow, and hey, it might even lead you to a certain person or exact situation you needed or dreamed of.

A saying that I love when it comes to this is, "every rejection is a redirection," or better yet, "every rejection is God's (the universe/higher source) protection."

Whatever resonates with you.

CHAPTER 2

LIE #2: BURNOUT IS "NORMAL"

"Burnout is what happens when you try to avoid being human for too long," – Michael Gungor

I was in agony.

Waves of unimaginable throbbing consumed my head, causing my vision to blur.

One moment, I was sitting in my office, typing away like usual.

The next, everything went foggy.

MEDICAL MYSTERY

Every story needs a character, right?

That's me.

Burnout. Dizziness. Pain.

Those are the 3 words I would use to describe that time.

A couple of years ago, I was working as a school counselor, which quickly became a highly stressful position.

Seriously, don't even think about underestimating the kind of pressure and responsibility that comes with managing the mental health of kids and teens.

On this note, I mean, could we just take a moment to appreciate all the social workers, nurses, teachers, counselors, and therapists out there?

These people deserve to be applauded and respected for all that they do. It's some of the most demanding jobs, emotionally and physically.

So, if you happen to be in a similar line of work, please look after yourself.

In my case, I was building the counseling department in the school from scratch as the school never had one before. And guess what? I was the only one in that department.

Yes, you read that right.

No team, no support staff, just me, myself, and I.

Talk about flying solo, right?

During that time, I was juggling a crazy amount of mental health cases from both primary and secondary school students. I'm talking double the students, double the workload, double the cases, and double the stress.

I was working with kids and teens dealing with depression, anxiety, self-harm, abuse, neglect, self-image issues, family problems, anger management, behavior concerns – you name it, I've seen it all.

But, I was not only managing all the students' mental health but also, on top of that, I provided support, tips and tools to the parents, teachers, and even the psychologists and psychiatrists who were treating the same students in external clinics.

My work hours *"should"* have been from 7:45am to 3:30pm, but I would show up before 6:45am and wouldn't leave until 6pm. That too, with no lunch breaks whatsoever as there were just so many students that needed my attention.

So, I dedicated myself to this job, going above and beyond. I spent my evenings and weekends working on student cases, constantly brainstorming ways to better support them as well as replying to endless emails.

It was a never-ending cycle.

The students, especially the children that I was working with were always on my mind and I had many sleepless nights thinking about how I can better support them.

I know, as counselors and therapists, we're supposed to prioritize our own mental health too, but over the months, I had become completely unaware of how work obsessed I had become.

My job took over my whole life. It became my identity.

Being the youngest person on the staff didn't help either. I felt this extra pressure to "prove" myself to everyone around me, especially since I've always had a baby face.

I mean, when I first started working, most of the teachers and parents thought I was a student!

I'm sure this will be a positive thing as I get older, but as someone who was just starting her new job, I wasn't really taken seriously. I was also unaware of a massive self-worth wound that required me to constantly seek validation from others that I was "doing a good job" and that I was "worthy."

All this stress, over time, took a toll on me.

My sleep went out the window, as did my eating and my mental health.

This eventually led to my body shutting down too.

One morning, I was sitting in my office when, out of nowhere, I felt this excruciating pain shooting through the back of my head.

It was like someone had zapped me with an electric shock.

My heart started racing like crazy and I was frozen in place for a few minutes.

What the hell was happening to me?

The electric pain slowly started to turn into this consistent, throbbing that took over the bottom half of my head and refused to stop.

I tried to brush it off. "Just ignore it," I kept saying to myself as I began to regain the muscle movements in my hand.

But it was impossible to ignore.

The pain was on a whole other level. I had never felt anything like it before.

As the days went by, the pulsating pain in my head got worse and worse. I ended up seeing every doctor and specialist for months. I visited countless consultants all over the country. My life became endless blood tests, X-rays, and scans, all in a desperate search for answers.

But they told me there was nothing "wrong" with me, physically.

I was apparently *fine*.

But I knew I was far from being fine.

This pain impacted my sleep, my vision, and my eating. I had to completely stop driving and got taken to the ER more times than I can count, because I kept feeling dizzy, sick, and light headed. I was confined to my bed, helpless and hopeless.

After a series of *more* scans on my head and body, a doctor dropped a bombshell: I was diagnosed with Osteoporosis.

But here's the kicker, he said that it was NOT the reason behind this excruciating pain in my head.

As if already having this unexplained pain at the back of my head, extreme fatigue, severe hormonal problems I was already dealing with at the time wasn't enough, here came a completely unrelated diagnosis.

The last thing I wanted was an additional diagnosis that had nothing to do with my current pain or symptoms.

And in case you're not familiar with Osteoporosis (I sure wasn't before all this happened), it's a disease that weakens your bones and is considered "incurable".

There's this one memory that sticks out in my mind from that time: when the doctor diagnosed me with osteoporosis, he told me this disease could eventually put me into a vegetative state and cut my life short.

I mean, I was in my early 20s at the time, thinking I had a whole lifetime of health, energy, and opportunities ahead of me.

Over the next few weeks, I just kept feeling worse and felt so sorry for myself.

Thinking back to this time, I realized that it was definitely one of the hardest for me and my family.

And I was slowly moving into the darkness of depression.

I didn't even want to get out of bed, because what was the point?

Why bother fighting this pain and this "incurable" diagnosis?

The years prior to this period, I had also been suffering with body dysmorphia, self-hate, and an extremely unhealthy relationship with food for over 17 years filled with restriction. And my body just couldn't take it anymore

But then one day, something shifted in me. I decided that enough was enough.

Sure, I had hit rock bottom. Yes, I was going through some serious emotional and physical pain. But life throws challenges and hardships at everyone, right?

There was no superhero coming to "save" me.

It was up to me to figure out how to live and heal.

That night, I grabbed my laptop in bed and went on a full-on Google spree. I wanted to know everything I could do with self-healing, and I was determined to find some answers to the mysterious pain I was experiencing, along with my hormonal problems, body image issues, and this new diagnosis of Osteoporosis.

After all my research, desperately browsing and consuming websites, blogs, books, and podcasts, I decided to try the alternative medicine route.

I went to practitioners specializing in Holistic Healing, Nutrition, Ayurveda, Acupuncture, Dry Cupping, Energy Healing, Hypnotherapy, and even did a session of Magnetic Field Therapy which involved using different kinds of magnets on the body.

Yes, Magnetic Field Therapy is real and an ACTUAL thing, believe it or not, and I went with my mum (which is a story for another time).

Through this journey, I discovered that this pain stemmed from a combination of emotional and physical imbalances. Turns out, years of neglecting myself, unhealed childhood wounds, having an unhealthy relationship with food, and running on pure burnout and external validation had taken a huge toll on my body.

My body was practically screaming at me to take a break.

You know what never sits right with me? In today's society, it's "normal" to be exhausted, drained, tired, fatigued, stressed, and just straight-up burned out. Especially for those of us stuck in soul-sucking jobs or dealing with stressful home lives.

And the worst part, people would tell me that my pain and burnout were all my fault because I was "too sensitive," and that's why I "couldn't handle a job." Which is obviously not the case.

It's absolutely ridiculous how society thinks being highly sensitive means you're "weak," when in reality, it's the exact opposite.

Sensitivity is courage.

I actually bought into that nonsense for quite a while, thinking I had to change who I was or toughen up to survive a "real job". That I had to stop being sensitive to be able to "handle a job".

But I have come to realize that it wasn't actually my "sensitivity" that was making me feel emotionally, mentally, and physically wrecked by a demanding job. No, it was just me **being human**, plain and simple.

We, as human beings, are not meant to live like this.

We are meant to breathe and not be chronically stressed.

We are meant to be free and not become another rat in the rat race.

Yet, most of us are currently stuck in this crazy cycle of stress, like we're trapped in a hamster wheel.

"Misery is the business model of the human race and we live it like marionettes on puppet strings. They got us enslaved or addicted to something: fast, TV, video games, social media, and just like good little rats, we go along with it, medicating our misery with whatever salvation they produce. And if we get fat or depressed medicating our emptiness? Well, the drug companies have a product to sell you too." – MJ DeMarco, Unscripted - The Great Rat-Race Escape

Why is burnout a problem for our physical bodies?

Our bodies are not used to the amount of stress that we face every day, as it perceives that as an actual threat. So, our bodies go into panic mode, thinking that these everyday stresses are life or death situations.

Whether it's something as mundane as being stuck in traffic or a work deadline, or even if it's just constantly worrying about losing our job or not making enough money to pay the bills, our body triggers the stress hormones.

Then the hypothalamus (a small region at the base of our brain) sets off an alarm and sends a warning to our nerves and hormones, telling our adrenal glands to release a large amount of stress hormones like cortisol and adrenaline. It's our body's way of signaling that it's "under attack".

It's these hormones that produce the physiological changes that we feel, like an increased heart rate, increased blood pressure, sweating, increased breathing, and muscle tenseness.

Cortisol (a stress hormone) suppresses "nonessential" systems in our bodies and shuts down our immune system, reproductive system, digestive system, and even our growth systems as we won't be "needing them" when we're too busy trying to survive or run away from danger.

This is why before an important exam, interview, or presentation, our immune system often doesn't work efficiently (thanks to our automatic stress response), so we become more susceptible to getting sick with the flu. I mean, I always got sick during exam season! Did you?

Similarly, as women, our hormonal systems go out of balance during a stressful period. When we're burned out or push ourselves and our bodies too hard, some of us women might not get our period for months, or even years!

These reactions to stress are known as the "fight-or-flight" response, which is the evolutionary survival mechanism that we have in our bodies. It's basically our body's way of helping us survive dangerous situations, and it helps us react quickly to life-threatening situations and predators so we either fight the threat or run to safety.

Back in the day, it was all about running away from lions and genuinely surviving real life threats. But now, in modern society, real life-threatening threats and predators are extremely rare.

So, whether it's a lion chasing you or an upcoming deadline, your body will react the same way. Even normal day to day stressors like when someone cuts you off in traffic, bills piling up, an angry dog that jumps out at you, family/relationship challenges, or when you're simply dealing with a horrible boss, make your body think that these things are actual threats to your survival.

This mechanism served us in the past. I mean, it helped us actually SURVIVE. That's why we are still here today. But when it comes to our current day to day and worrying about the little things, it's no longer serving us.

And as a result, our body's stress response system is always activated.

This constant stress has turned us into a society that's become addicted to certain emotions, and it's taking a toll on our mental and physical well-being, leading to burnout.

Tony Robbins calls this addiction of emotions our "emotional homes" – which are the feelings and emotions that we constantly feel and go back to as our default baseline. And more often than not, they are not positive.

Your emotional home is basically the place where you feel super comfortable and always end up going back to. And yes, it's not always the healthiest place to be. But it's familiar and kind of like a habit.

For example, if you grew up in an environment that is toxic and unhealthy, you will most likely find yourself having equally toxic relationships in adulthood. Because, deep down, having that kind of connection feels like home to you. It's like reliving the same dynamic you had with your parents or guardian. You might feel "good" in that place, but it's not healthy.

You feel safe in your emotional home, even if it's unhealthy and negative, simply because it feels familiar to you. So, having a healthy relationship with someone might throw you off because you're not used to that, or you think you don't deserve that, if you've only been in unhealthy relationships all your life.

It's the same for our emotions.

Doubt, anxiety, fear, anger, frustration, and overwhelm tend to be our go-to emotions.

Living with this long-term stress is like opening a door to a whole bunch of health issues. It disrupts our bodies in every way imaginable, increasing the risk of anxiety, depression, headaches, low mood, weight problems, lack of focus, memory issues, cancer, heart diseases, heart attacks, strokes, high blood pressure, physical pain, and the list goes on.

I recently conducted a little survey on my Instagram (@inspirewithyas if you haven't followed me yet…seriously, what are you doing?!), asking my community consisting of women aged 18-35 how often they feel burned out or stressed. And the results? **90%** of them were experiencing burnout and stress **every single day.**

Now, doesn't that say something about the state of things?

There is something fundamentally wrong here.

This can't be normal.

Feeling stressed and overwhelmed has somehow become the standard.

I feel this stems from the toxic mentality ingrained in our society, promoting the "go hard or go home," "no time to rest," and "rest is for the dead" type of programming.

This hustle culture pushes our bodies toward fight or flight, which ends up shutting down our creative brain centers and every bodily system that is literally keeping us healthy and alive.

Hustle culture is a never-ending cycle of stress with skyrocketing cortisol levels, and it's seriously harming our mental and physical well-being.

After hitting my own rock bottom and finally getting out of it, I created a FREE Self-Care Planner that was part of my morning ritual. The questions and tips I give in this planner are what really helped me begin my healing journey.

Using this planner will allow you to reconnect with your heart, body, and soul and give yourself what you need FIRST every morning before giving away your energy to the chaos of the day (my clients also use this and it's helped them too).

Use this planner to reconnect with your true self and continue to guide you on this journey of self-discovery while you read this book.

You can download it for FREE on

www.inspirewithyas.com/selfcare

"I'M SO TIRED"

Have you realized how saying "I'm so tired" has become such a normal thing to say?

When people ask how we're doing, we automatically reply with "tired" or "busy," right?

But how many of us would actually say, "I'm feeling energized, fantastic, radiant?"

Not many, I bet.

And even if someone did say that, most people would think they're weird, crazy, and strange.

I believe that society instilled this belief that if we're not overwhelmed, burned out, or chronically tired, then we're just not working hard enough.

But that's totally wrong.

Here's an excerpt from Shonda Rhimes' book, The Year of Yes, talking about burnout, especially when it comes to mothers:

"I am on Twitter, checking in on the world, and I see a tweet from some motherhood site. It says: "Sleeplessness is a badge of honor for moms."

What?

A badge of honor?

Right then and there, my hair catches on fire. My hair just lights up in flames of instant rage. The rage may be especially bad because I still have some PTSD from my oldest child's infant days.

My perfect beautiful miracle baby?

Never slept. EVER. Never.

Twelve years later, the memories of those nights, of that sleep deprivation, still make me rock back and forth a little bit. You want to torture someone? Hand them an adorable baby they love who doesn't sleep.

Badge of honor?

Necessarily evil, yes. Pain in the ass, yes.

Badge of honor?

Are you freaking kidding me? Who believes that crap? Who is drinking THAT crazy Kool-Aid?

But a lot of people are. MOST people are.

I don't think it ever occurred to me before how much and how often women are praised for displaying traits that basically render them invisible. When I really think about it, I realize the culprit is the language generally used to praise women. Especially mothers.

"She sacrificed everything for her children... She never thought about herself... She gave up everything for us... She worked tirelessly to make sure we had what we needed. She stood in the shadows, she was the wind beneath our wings."

Greeting cards companies are built on that idea.

"Tell her how much all the little things she does all year long that seem to go unnoticed really mean to you."

With a $2.59 card.

Mother's Day is built on that idea.

This is good, we're told. It's good how Mom diminishes and martyrs herself. The message is: mothers, you are such wonderful and good people because you make yourselves smaller, because you deny your own needs, because you toil tirelessly in the shadows and no one ever thanks or notices you…this all makes you AMAZING.

Yuck.

What the hell kind of message is that?

Would ANYONE praise a man for this?

These are not behaviors anyone would hope to instill in their daughters, right?

Right?

I'm not saying MOTHERHOOD shouldn't be praised. Motherhood should be praised. Motherhood is wonderful. I'm doing it. I think it's great.

There are all kinds of ways and reasons that mothers can and should be praised. But for cultivating a sense of invisibility, martyrdom and tirelessly working unnoticed and unsung? Those are not reasons.

Praise women for standing in the shadows?

Wrong."

This above piece just goes to show how burnout has become the "norm" and is even celebrated, especially with moms.

Now, the crazy thing?

Burnout doesn't only come from your job or the responsibilities you have at home. It can also creep up when you let other people control your day and tell you what you "should" be doing.

Even those so-called "internet gurus" who claim to have all the answers and know all the secrets on how to live your "best life" can contribute to burnout and stress.

They'll preach about how much sleep you *should* get, when you *should* wake up, what you *should* eat, what time you *should* eat it, how much you *should* eat, how you *should* work out, and how you *should* spend every single minute of your every single day.

Let's be clear here, I listen to experts and continually learn from them. But blindly following their advice and 4 am morning routines without checking in with yourself, your own needs, your intuition, your own body, or what your capabilities are… is where the problem lies.

We are all unique individuals, and there's no "one size fits all" approach that works for everyone.

Trust me, this only adds extra, unnecessary stress and fuels your burnout even more when you stop listening to what your body truly needs.

When I followed a strict diet and an extreme workout routine, I ended up adding more stress onto my body, which made me gain weight instead of losing it, and my skin was like a minefield of spots. And don't even get me started on my terrible mental health and zero energy levels during that time.

I never took the time to rest when my body needed it, or to fuel up when it was begging for food. I was just blindly following what everyone else said ***should*** work for my health and weight loss.

But you know what?

The key takeaway here is that you don't have to let society, your job, your boss, gurus, or those "influencers" have complete power over your mental health, sleep, food, or physical well-being.

Instead of giving them the control, keep it to yourself. Take advice but always check in with yourself and see what feels right first.

It's time to start reconnecting with yourself, and take full responsibility for your current life.

In the book, Unscripted - The Great Rat-Race Escape by MJ DeMarco, the author talks about how you can take charge of your happiness. They're called Happiness Levers, and here's a quick overview of what they are:

1. Gratitude

2. Autonomy (making your own decisions and choices)

3. Purpose (having a mission outside of yourself)

4. Physical Health.

Health is **real wealth** in the end.

Without your health, you have nothing.

I remember seeing Steven Bartlett, the host of the Diary of a CEO podcast, during a talk in an Entrepreneurial Festival here in the United Arab Emirates. He talked about how our physical health is the foundation of everything and used the table in front of him on stage as an example.

If a table wasn't solid or strong, how can we expect to put things on top of it? It's the same with our health. If we're not in a good place health-wise, how can we expect to focus on building a beautiful life for ourselves?

Also, in the book Choose Happy by Sarah Gregg, the author also talks about the power of gratitude and how we get to CHOOSE happiness. It's a decision that we have to make every day, not something we can get just by sitting around, waiting for it to happen without any work.

The problem is how most of us tend to wait for happiness to come from the outside, our circumstances or external stimuli, like buying fancy things or getting a promotion.

But this simply makes us powerless.

HOW TO BREAK FREE

1. **Stop wearing burnout like a badge of honor (plus it's time to add some boundaries).**

   The world we currently live in is so fast paced and prioritizes "result" over anything else.

   It seems like nowadays, everyone's running around at lightning speed, obsessed with getting results. But here's the thing: results aren't always in our control. That's up to a higher power, whether you call it God, the Universe, Source energy, or something else that resonates with you.

What we can control, though, is how we prioritize our own mental health with our input and actions.

It's time to stop stressing about the outcomes that we're waiting for.

Will worrying actually change what's meant for us? No.

Will it change something that's not meant for us? Also no.

What's meant to be will find its way to us, no matter what.

So, remember this: nothing in this world is worth sacrificing your peace of mind or your health. Especially not your job.

And that is why setting boundaries is absolutely crucial.

During a Theta healing training I was doing, the teacher said something that really stuck with me. They said that we do things either **out of duty or out of love**.

That really got me thinking. What does it mean?

I started looking at all the things I was committed to and where I put most of my time and energy. And I asked myself, am I doing these things because I love them or just out of duty? Turns out, a lot of it was out of duty. Because I felt obligated to do them.

Now, reconsider some of the things that you are committed to. Think about your plate.

Where does the majority of your attention, energy, and time go? And are you doing those actions **out of love** or **out of duty?**

If it's the latter, then maybe it's time to set some boundaries and start saying NO more often. And here's a trick: instead of straight-up saying no, you can respond with "I'll think about it and get back to you."

This simple response has given me, a shy and introverted recovering people pleaser, the space to think and respond in a way that suits me and my own priorities. It gives me some time to really think about whether I want to do something or not.

No more feeling pressured into saying yes when I really didn't want to, just because I can't think of an excuse on the spot.

So, now it's your turn. Give it a shot. Say NO or "I'll think about it." It will give you a chance to step back, re-evaluate your priorities, and stop doing things that you don't want to do. And this can make a world of difference in how stressed and burned out you feel, since you will no longer be doing things that you feel forced or don't want to do.

2. **Your time is the most valuable asset that you have.**

   Act like it.

Take a look at the people you're hanging out with.

What type of people are they?

Are they draining, negative, and toxic? Do they just suck the life out of you?

How do you feel once you finally escape their clutches?

Do they inspire you or support you or get you all excited?

If not, it's time to start putting limits on the time you spend with them. Even if they're a part of your family (I mean, being related by blood doesn't automatically mean that you have to put up with their toxicity).

I know it's not easy. I know it's easier said than done. But hey, as a super sensitive empath and a recovering people pleaser, I totally get the struggle of saying no, tolerating toxic behaviors and environments.

The first step in becoming the person you want to be is realizing just how valuable your time and energy are. Letting someone drain you is like betraying yourself. And eventually, your physical and mental health will also suffer.

Allow me to say this because no one else will – you don't have to respond right away!

With our constant connection to each other every single minute of every single day, society has created this expectation that we should always be available to respond to messages and calls right away.

But you don't really have to do that.

Give yourself some breathing room.

Don't feel pressured to reply until you're mentally ready.

Know that you *can* give yourself the space to disconnect and respond when you have the mental capacity to. Personally, I like to set aside a specific time each day to go through all my messages (unless it's family or something urgent) and get back to them.

Reacting right away can create so much stress. It's impossible to always "be" there for everyone 24/7.

So, don't beat yourself up about it.

You're a human, not a robot.

3. **State management.**

Change your physiology. Change your life.

"Emotions are motions in energy," – Tony Robbins

Your physiology plays a massive role in your emotional state. Tony Robbins often talks about this and constantly emphasizes the importance of starting your day by doing something physical to change your state of mind.

It could be stretching, meditating, running, walking, or even yoga.

Moving your body is one of the quickest ways to change your state of mind.

The famous saying that "you're only one workout away from a good mood" is pretty spot on. But even something as simple as a walk can go a long way.

I've been incorporating walking after dinner for the past year and it's seriously boosted my mood and my sleep. And hey, you might have heard about Amy Cuddy, the author of Presence. She gave a TED talk that got a staggering 52 million views, where she talked about how striking a superhero pose or simply changing your posture can be extremely powerful.

"Movement, like posture, tells the brain how it feels and even manages what it remembers. As walking becomes more open, upright, and buoyant, our memories about ourselves follow suit," – Amy Cuddy

CHAPTER 3
LIE #3: TRADITIONAL EDUCATION EMPOWERS YOU

"Education is not the filling of a pail, but the lighting of a fire," – William Butler Yeats

Well. You better forget and unlearn a majority of what you were taught in the traditional education system.

Because I have found that true learning actually happens after graduation.

The education system deeply affects our sense of identity, creativity, strengths, and mental abilities, but not in a positive way.

There is a vast universe out there that we still know so little about.

There are mountains and mountains of knowledge that remain undiscovered.

Despite claiming to know so much, we truly know very little in the grand scheme of things.

This realization is quite humbling, if I may say so myself.

We've barely scratched the surface of what intelligence and knowledge are out there.

And more importantly, we've barely scratched the surface of the intelligence, potential, and power that lies dormant within us. It's all within you, waiting to be unleashed.

Yet, many of us believe we "have it all figured out and know everything", but let these two quotes from Thomas Edison sum it up:

"It's obvious that we don't know one millionth of one percent of anything."

"Fools call wise men fools. A wise man never calls any man a fool."

Now, if you search up Thomas Edison on Google, you'll find this little blurb about him: "Edison was famous for never giving up in his search for the construction of the electric light bulb. Without his tenacity and almost hard-headed way of never giving up, his idea may not have ever come to fruition."

But wait.

Let's dig a little deeper into this.

Turns out, Edison wasn't actually the first person to invent the light bulb!

Strange, right?

So, why were we taught that he did?

Well, don't worry, we'll get into that later.

But before we go any further, let's go a little back.

Our education system has been around for about 200 years now, and it was mainly reserved "exclusively" for the elite. But then industrialization happened, and suddenly we needed schools to pump out workers for the industry.

Yes, you read that right.

The whole purpose of our school system was to create factory workers.

It's been said time and time again that traditional schooling is all about churning out obedient workers, not independent thinkers.

See, back in the day, factory owners wanted employees who would follow orders, show up on time, and do as they were told. So, sitting on the same desk and chair in a cold classroom, listening to a teacher talk for 7 hours a day was considered perfect training for factory work.

But, now, we've come a long way since those industrial days. This educational system may have served the industrial society at that time, but we are no longer in that period.

I mean, just look at where we are now. It's a completely new era. We've got technology that does pretty much everything, from AI machines to robots and hey, even flying cars! Medicine has also come a long way. Same with engineering and dentistry.

Everything has evolved over the years, but guess what?

Our education system is still stuck in the same old rut. It's the only thing that hasn't changed.

Why is that?

Well, according to Johann Gottlieb Fichte, a German philosopher, *"education should aim at destroying free will, so that, after pupils have left school, they shall be incapable, throughout the rest of their lives, of thinking or acting otherwise than as their schoolmasters would have wished."*

So, has the traditional schooling system actually achieved this aim?

I'll let you decide that.

I mean, why are we learning quadratic equations? Pythagoras? Algebra?

I've never used algebra in my life and I doubt you have either.

Instead of teaching us useless math concepts, why didn't school focus on teaching us practical skills like building relationships? Entrepreneurial skills? Negotiation skills? Crisis management? Investment? Taxes? Bills? Emotional intelligence? Mental health?

Well, I believe it's because these are the skills that actually enhance our daily lives and they were intentionally left out of our education.

It's like what the American journalist H.L. Mencken said:

"What is the purpose of industrial education? To fill the young of the species with knowledge and awaken their intelligence? Nothing could be further from the truth. The aim is simply to reduce as many individuals as possible to the same safe level, to breed and train a standardized citizenry, to put down dissent and originality."

In high school, I remember having a subject called Life Skills. Sounds great, but spoiler alert: It was a complete joke. There were no life skills taught throughout the years we took this mandatory class in school. Funny, isn't it?

Even the subject I took, Business and Communications (BACS), in my GCSE year turned out to be a waste of time. I took the subject since I thought it was an "easy A" but even then, I honestly thought that maybe, just maybe, I would learn a useful thing or two but sadly not. As expected, I came out of the class with no new skills, no new business OR communication skills, but well, at least I did get the A.

This is why I believe it's so important for us to RETHINK and question what is normal in our society, and why things are the way they are.

Just like what Adam Grant talks about in his book Think Again.

This quote from his book sums this up quite well:

"We instantly believe what teachers teach us. We believed that Pluto was a planet. Cleopatra was Egyptian. But after years in the education, there's been a lot that has been found and discovered. There's a lot of hidden history. Certain pieces of history that wasn't given to us for a reason. To hide ideas that may empower us or make us question things."

Doesn't this make you wonder if we were fed with a polished "fake" version of history instead of what actually went down?

Throughout time, Astrology has gotten a bad reputation thanks to those teenage girl magazines using it to see if their high school crush was their soulmate, or if you were going to get zapped by lightning for crossing paths with a black cat.

Astrology in mainstream magazines and websites were also used to "predict" if you would have a "bad week" all based solely on your star sign.

So, unfortunately over the years, Astrology became a big joke filled with nonsense fluff.

But you know what? There is a whole other side to Astrology that's been kept under wraps. It takes an entirely different approach and was not made mainstream.

If used and understood correctly, Astrology can actually help us understand ourselves on a deep level, whether that's digging into our psyche, spirituality, or mental state.

The ancient Egyptian, Greek, and Babylonian civilizations all used Astrology to gain wisdom and knowledge. It was a major part of their development and learning. There is also a branch of Astrology called Electional Astrology, or Event Astrology, where they pick the perfect time for an event based on the stars.

And Astrology isn't the only thing that's been hidden from us. There are tons of ancient civilizations out there proving that humans had some serious potential, skills, and technology that they can tap into. Look into what any of the ancient civilizations have built – there are so many books (Graham Hancock's books are great on this) and documentaries that shed light on the true extent of our human capabilities.

But instead, what did school do? Waste our time in school learning about King Henry and his merry band of wives. How informative.

For a long time, we've just gone along with what we were told about the people who supposedly changed the world with their ideas. But these stories are based on **imprecise sources**. We learn so much about different people and their knowledge that changed our lives forever, but have we ever stopped to question if these stories are accurate?

Now, humor me for a minute and let's take a look at some so-called "facts" that most of us have been taught to be true.

Thomas Edison invented the electric light.

FALSE.

Turns out it was actually a couple of not-so-famous discoverers named Humphrey Davy and Joseph Swan who deserve the credit. Fun fact: They even won a patent lawsuit against Edison!

Pasta originated from Italy.

FALSE.

Food historians believe that it actually originated from the Arab world, specifically Libya.

A goldfish has a 3-second memory.

FALSE.

Well, according to some research conducted by the School of Psychology in 2003, that's not the case at all. They can and do remember things for weeks, months, or even years.

Chameleons change color to blend in with their surroundings.

FALSE.

It's actually based on their mood, not the environment.

Fortune cookies originated from China.

FALSE.

They actually originated in the US thanks to a Japanese immigrant in the late 19th or early 20th century.

Newcomen invented the first steam engine.

FALSE.

It was actually first created by Heron from Alexandria, Egypt.

Cleopatra was Egyptian.

FALSE.

She was actually Greek.

Glass originated from China.

FALSE.

Archaeologists found glass artifacts dating back to ancient Egypt in 1350 BC.

"In education, after revelations in history and revolutions in science, it often takes years for a curriculum to be updated and textbooks to be revised. Researchers have recently discovered that we need to rethink widely accepted assumptions," – Adam Grant, Think Again

So, what's the deal with these "facts"? Well, it seems like the stories of their origins aren't necessarily based on solid historical evidence. Instead, they are shaped by hidden agendas, market trends, and the good old-fashioned popularity.

But hey, despite all that, the traditional schooling system still keeps teaching these inaccurate pieces of information as absolute truths.

Go figure!

EXTRAVERT VS INTROVERT

A lot of people think that you have to be extraverted to be successful, but that's just another lie.

In this book called Quiet by Susan Cain, she talks about how being an introvert is not wrong or limiting you. She believes that introverts are often deep thinkers. They might hate small talk but they are more creative and intuitive.

Introverts are also highly emotional and empathetic, which makes them experience the emotions of others and their own at a deeper and more intense level. And that is why they are really observant too, noticing all the little details that others might miss.

"At school you might have been prodded to come "out of your shell" – that noxious expression which fails to appreciate that some animals naturally carry shelter everywhere they go, and that some humans are just the same," – Susan Cain, Quiet

We all have our own unique personality traits that make us who we are. You could be someone who is more outgoing and extraverted, while others tend to be more introverted. In any case, there's nothing wrong with you.

Being introverted is nothing to be ashamed of – it's simply a part of who we are.

As an introvert, you may have even often gotten mistaken and misunderstood for being shy or "anti-social", but introversion is not shyness. It's about finding energy and solace in solitude. It's about being comfortable in smaller gatherings over large social events. It's about being able to recharge by spending time alone.

In a society that values extraversion and social interaction, it's important to recognize and appreciate the unique strengths that introverts bring to the table.

You see, being introverted is generally frowned upon in the school system, corporate world, and social circles. Most schools prioritize and glamorize the confident and outgoing individuals. They teach us that being loud and extraverted is what matters and is what's "right". Even group assignments and presentations are designed to favor extraverts rather than introverts.

However, I'd like to point out that nobody is purely introverted or extraverted all the time.

I believe we all fall somewhere on the spectrum, depending on the situation, the people around us, or even our mood on a particular day.

I mean, I personally lean more toward introversion, but that doesn't mean I can't tap into my extraverted side when necessary!

The problem lies in society's tendency to categorize people as either ONE or the other. You can be either an introvert OR an extravert, as if being more introverted automatically means you're doomed to a life devoid of success or any form of confidence.

When I worked as a school counselor, every so often there would be some kids who got flagged as a "concern". The teachers would get worried about them as these kids were a little socially withdrawn, didn't have many friends, and preferred to do their own thing like reading, drawing, or simply being by themselves rather than hanging out with the other kids.

The teachers and parents were all up in arms about their "social" intelligence and abilities, and whether they could make friends. But when I talked to these kids, it turned out they weren't "shy" or socially awkward at all.

They were just making a choice – they were CHOOSING to not socialize.

They were CHOOSING not to talk to other kids because they weren't interested in their conversations or the topics they were into.

They were CHOOSING to spend time alone, doing what they loved.

And you know what?

That's perfectly OK.

There's a difference between children who used to be extremely social and extraverted, and suddenly became withdrawn. That's a different matter. I'm talking about the children who are naturally more introverted.

The pressure that we put on these kids in traditional schools to always be speaking up and putting themselves out there can be extremely overwhelming. It's especially so for the introverted and withdrawn ones.

And here's the thing, these children have a variety of other skills and strengths that traditional schooling doesn't even bother to consider or help them develop.

It's just like that quote: *"Everyone is a genius. But if you judge a fish by its ability to climb a tree, it will live its whole life believing that it is stupid." – Unknown*

So, let this be a little reminder that you are perfect just the way you are, being your natural self. There is no direct link between success and being extraverted.

You can be a leader, a change maker, or even a CEO as an introvert.

Don't let society's rules hold you back any longer.

You can achieve whatever level of success you want no matter what, and true confidence is a SKILL that you can learn and practice. It's like a muscle, the more you exercise it, the stronger it gets.

ARE WE BORN GENIUSES?

According to a new study, when kids are young, most of them show signs of being creative geniuses.

But here's the catch: as they grow up, those numbers drop drastically.

Back in 1968, according to NASA standards, a study by George Land and Beth Jarman found that **98%** of children were creative geniuses! But as time went on, that number plummeted. By the age of 10, it was down to 30%, by 15 it dropped to 12%, and by adulthood, it was a measly 2%. Crazy, isn't it?

Now, we have researchers at Birkbeck University in London who are trying to dig deeper into this whole creativity thing. They're using brainwave scanning caps to see what's going on inside kids' brains while they do different tasks.

Artie Wu, who is an expert on parenting and relationships, has shared his own thoughts on this topic. He says that when kids are little, they see the world as it is, without any filter. They are already like little geniuses. They see everything for what it truly is and they are not afraid to speak their minds.

But us adults, we lose that over time. We have to go through the whole "trimming, training, and educating" process to fit into society. And apparently, we do that by shaming kids.

NASA's test for creative genius was all about thinking outside the box, or as they call it, "divergent thinking." Kids are natural at that, but when we get older, we get scared of being wrong, so we hold back these crazy ideas. It's a whole shame vs guilt thing. Shame makes us feel like there's something fundamentally wrong with us, while guilt is more like a mistake that we can fix.

And shame, well, it messes with children's heads.

They feel like they're not loved as much because of it.

Imagine what it would be like if we were encouraged instead of shamed as kids.

There's this story about young Picasso, the famous artist. The gist of it is: his father saw how good he was at painting and offered him his own brushes, declaring him the new family painter.

So, here's the big question: what if we all have this inner Picasso inside us, and it's just waiting to be unleashed? That's what Artie believes, and honestly, it sounds pretty fascinating.

The same researchers at Birkbeck University are hoping to use their brain scanning tech on adults too, and who knows, they might just uncover the genius that's hiding inside all of us.

THE BIGGEST LIE

Now, comes one of the biggest lies we're fed in the traditional education system…

That going to university automatically scores you a great job and career instantly.

Let's take a moment to really think about this, shall we?

We have all herded into this **outdated** educational system and brainwashed into believing that university is the ultimate goal, the key to achieving our dreams (or our parents' dreams).

But the majority of university graduates end up right back where they started: feeling lost, confused, and stressed, but now with a lovely side dish of student debt.

We were sold on this idea that going to university "guarantees" us a job. But let me tell you, now more than ever, this is one of the BIGGEST lies perpetuated by formal education.

"Earn a university degree and land yourself a great job."

That's what we all bought into, and for a period of time, it did work **moderately**. But nowadays, in many fields, this guarantee is nothing but a load of nonsense.

Yet, society keeps pushing it.

Parents keep pushing it.

Culture keeps pushing it.

And unfortunately, in many cultures, it's crazy that there's even shame surrounding individuals who didn't go to university!

My parents moved us from Egypt to the UK when I was just a 5-month-old baby and was raised there my whole life. They always reminded us that they came to this country for the sole purpose of providing us with a good education and the opportunity to attend great universities.

I am truly grateful for that, and I know that many of you who have immigrant parents or grandparents can relate to the hardships they endured to ensure our families had access to the best education, resources, and a safe environment to grow in.

However, it is important for families and cultures to begin to recognize that traditional university may not be the only path to success, but that success can be achieved through many other routes.

When I asked members of my online community, @inspirewithyas, for their opinions on this matter, the majority shared stories of how they are not working in the field that they studied in university and considered their education a "waste of time." Yet, many others found success by entering the workforce, apprenticeships, or training opportunities directly after high school. Some found success through online platforms such as blogs and social media, affiliate marketing, virtual assistance, freelancing, e-commerce, online businesses, and so much more.

(Side note: I want to clarify that this does not apply to university subjects that require specific skills or hands-on training, such as medicine, pharmacy, dentistry, or engineering. etc.)

WHERE DID OUR CREATIVITY GO?

Now, another lie we're given within our traditional education system is that it tends to suppress our innate creativity and curiosity. An interesting article on Gaia.com confirms this:

"As children, we're born with wild and inventive imaginations. In fact, 98 percent of children are born creative geniuses according to a test devised by NASA scientists. But as we get older that figure dwindles, and by adulthood, the number of creative geniuses drops to an astonishingly low average.

When the deputy director of NASA wanted to figure out how to separate creative types from the rest, he tapped George Land to create a test. The goal was to seclude those who could think outside the box and come up with atypical solutions to some of NASA's toughest problems. So, in 1968, he created a test that accurately predicted creativity, but then found himself faced with the question of where creativity comes from. Is it learned, or does it come from experience?

Land decided to apply his test to a range of age groups to see how creativity varied as we get older. He used a sample of 1,600 children and continued the study into his subjects' adulthood. Incredibly, he found that by the time they reached maturity, only two percent of subjects passed the creativity test, despite their creative success as kids."

Ken Robinson, a renowned creativity expert known for his widely-watched TED talk, has challenged the traditional education system and advocated for a significant overhaul to promote creativity. He emphasizes the importance of recognizing different types of intelligence.

The Gaia.com article further highlights the need to prioritize creativity in education and how *"Robinson noticed that our education system teaches us that being wrong is the worst possible outcome.*

...our thought process is forced to conform to controlled paradigms of right and wrong, and so ideas that don't fit the mold are rejected. And in the past few decades, prescribing drugs to children who don't easily fall in line with the system's ideal standards has been "normalized".

Robinson points to the example of Gillian Lynne, one of the most famous theater choreographers who's made millions of her work on Broadway shows, including Cats and Phantom of the Opera. When she was a child she struggled with school and was told she had a learning disorder. Her parents took her to a doctor to figure out what was wrong and potentially prescribe her medication. The doctor told them she wasn't sick, she just needed to pursue dancing. And the rest is history.

Imagine how many dancers, artists, and creative types have had their potentials wasted because our system doesn't have the time or patience to guide them in the right direction. Instead, we're disciplined to follow narrow paths and if we don't conform, we're told that we failed.

...education, he says, is not the same as learning, learning requires engagement and sparked curiosity."

This article then goes on to say that "traditional teaching methods, like testing and memorization, were less than worthless. These systems were counterproductive to creativity and forced students to think linearly when instead they should be thinking in a non-linear manner."

We must now begin to realize that creativity is as essential as literacy and treat it with the same urgency and importance.

To echo this statement, the book Rich Dad Poor Dad emphasizes the significance of creativity by stating:

"Mike and I couldn't go along with the standard dogma our teachers preached, and that caused problems. Whenever the teacher said, "if you don't get good grades, you won't do well in *the real world," Mike and I just raised our eyebrows. When we were told to follow set procedures and not deviate from the rules, we could see how school discouraged creativity. We started to understand why our rich dad told us that schools were designed to produce good employees, instead of employers."*

What your teachers say isn't always the truth.

Another thing that seriously needs revising in our traditional education system is the idea that we have to blindly accept everything teachers say as the absolute truth. Which then becomes our reality.

How many times has a teacher called you a failure, a loud mouth, not that smart, a terrible writer, or just a jokester, and those labels have stuck with you ever since?

Unfortunately, many of us are programmed to blindly follow authority, just like in Milgram's experiment back in 1963. If you haven't heard of it, here's a quick rundown:

Social psychologist Stanley Milgram wanted to see how people justify committing horrible acts like genocide offered by those during World War II, so he researched the effect of authority of obedience.

In the original baseline study, he did this experiment where the authority figure wore a lab coat and surprise, surprise, people were more obedient.

But when an "ordinary member of the public" took over and ditched the lab coat, wearing everyday clothes instead, the obedience level dropped by 20%.

What does this tell us? That we're more likely to blindly follow authority figures or anyone who looks and dresses the part, and take whatever they say as the truth. But just because they are an authority or are wearing a "lab coat" doesn't mean they know better.

Let me share a little inspiring story with you.

My best friend in high school was constantly told by her teachers that she would never make it to university. They put her in the lower sets of classes, set a limit on what grades she could achieve, and capped her at a C grade, no matter how hard she worked.

At first, she doubted herself and was about to give up, until something shifted inside her. She knew deep down that she didn't accept these false restrictions on her life. No one will decide her fate but her!

So, she rejected these limitations of her potential and worked harder than anyone ever did, all the while convincing teachers to move her class sets up until she ended up with higher grades that got her into university!

And guess what?

She's a teacher now, at the same high school she and I both went to!

She was the first person in her whole family line to go to university.

She's out there inspiring students to break through the limitations and the glass ceiling.

She's a true inspiration.

So, now you've seen the other side of the traditional schooling system. I'm not saying it's all terrible and negative, and that we should just throw formal education out the window. I just think it's high time we give the traditional education system a much-needed revision.

HOW TO BREAK FREE

1. **Accept that you're allowed to make mistakes.**

    Have you realized how the traditional education system makes such a big fuss about getting and doing everything right? It teaches us that being wrong is the worst possible outcome. But when our thought process is forced to obey the paradigms of right and wrong, ideas that don't fit in are rejected.

    But you know what? Some of the best ideas come from a lot of bad ones, from messing up a bunch of times. I think many of us hold ourselves back from reaching our potential because we're so scared of being wrong or being labeled as a "failure".

    I'm not going to say the cliché thing that "there is no such thing as failure", but instead what I'm going to say is that failure only happens when you give up. And even when you do "fail", you're actually getting closer to achieving your goals!

    So, embrace those mistakes and failures, despite what school told you.

2. **Don't just assume this physical reality is all there is.**

You have to open your mind to the possibility that there's more to this reality than meets the eye.

Just because we were only introduced to our five senses, the Newtonian physics (basic physics focusing on gravity and matter) doesn't mean that there is so much wisdom out there ready for you to learn and utilize.

Seriously, look up Bruce Lipton and his mind-blowing research on all the hidden sides of physics, like Quantum Physics. It will blow your mind. There's a whole world out there that we haven't been told about!

What you see isn't all there is.

3. **Tap back into your creativity AND curiosity.**

So, here's the deal. The schooling system is all about sticking to the rules and killing off our inbuilt human strengths and qualities like curiosity, wonder, creativity, and connection to our intuition. School completely dims them down, if you ask me.

So, let's be rebels and tap back into those amazing human qualities and embrace creativity again! It's an unlearning process. Forget about all those assumptions and beliefs that have been drilled into your brain and start fresh. Let your gut be your guide, because creativity is already in you.

If you hear that little whisper telling you to try something new…follow it. BEFORE your logical rational conscious mind kicks in and makes you second guess it.

And if you want to really boost your creativity, hang out with other creative people, join a class you've been eyeing, or find an online group.

Let your creative adventures begin!

4. **Don't let anyone tell you what you are capable of.**

Only you have the power to decide what you can achieve. Only you can dictate your own capabilities. Think about your biggest "impossible" dream and know that you can accomplish it a thousand times over.

Countless everyday individuals have shattered boundaries and reached new heights, not just famous figures like JK Rowling, Walt Disney, or my best friend.

Each one of us has faced challenges and still accomplished things that seemed "impossible" at the time, even in the face of labels and diagnoses.

And can I just say, even if you're a woman who is marginalized and underrepresented like an Arab, Asian, Latino, or Black woman, don't let society specifically tell you that you're not capable of achieving what your fellow classmates or friends who come from a white privilege background can. Don't let that determine your level of success. You can achieve and do so much more as you have generations relying on you to break the boundaries and limitations.

(Side note: If you want some extra inspiration, there's a book called "The Spark: A Mother's Story of Nurturing, Genius, and Autism" about a boy named Jacob who was diagnosed with Autism at the age of 2 but went on to have an IQ higher than Einstein's, a photographic memory, and taught himself calculus in just two weeks.

By the age of 9, he was working on an original theory in astrophysics that experts believe could one day earn him a Nobel Prize.

At age 12, he became a paid researcher in quantum physics.)

Here's a small personal example: I struggled with stuttering as I grew up, and was told that it was something I would have to just live with. But with speech therapy and the unwavering support of my parents, who treated me no differently and refused to let me lose hope, I overcame it.

Plus, don't forget that I'm an Egyptian Muslim… I mean, the odds were definitely stacked against me.

So please, don't allow anyone to define your abilities or limitations.

You have the power to break boundaries.

5. **Give personality tests a try.**

   Taking the time to understand yourself, your partner, and your children on a deeper level is incredibly important.

   You can do this by engaging in learning tests and personality assessments. Personality tests for kids can help you, as a parent or guardian, uncover the best ways to connect with, understand, and motivate your child both in school and in life in general.

   These tests, along with seeking guidance from experts, can enhance your awareness of your own and your child's learning styles, allowing you to cater to them individually.

However, remember not to take these tests too seriously, as human beings are complex. They can serve as helpful guides, though.

Here are a few recommended personality tests to try out (and they're actually quite fun!):

- Myers-Briggs Type Indicator
- Enneagram (9 personality types)
- Big Five Assessment

And if you're feeling curious, explore your Astrology birth chart and Human Design. They are so interesting!

CHAPTER 4

LIE #4: WORKING THE 9-5 IS THE ONLY WAY TO ACHIEVE SUCCESS

"It's like we're dropped into this world and told that we are free. But we aren't free and it's just a lie. Because the world itself is a brilliant scheme to keep you working, spending and saving. And when you're smart enough to figure that out, scam advertises a new way to escape, but it doesn't help you escape. It keeps you in it. Grows tighter the harder you try," – MJ DeMarco, Unscripted - The Great Rat-Race Escape

Society loves cashing in on our pain and misery. It profits from our trauma and depression.

The more they keep us stuck in survival mode, the more we're trapped in this never-ending rat race.

We're too busy just trying to survive that we don't have any room or energy left to even think about thriving.

HERE'S THE DEAL.

Before we dive in, let's get one thing straight. I'm not here to dismiss all those 9-5 jobs in this chapter. Nor am I saying that this system doesn't work for some people.

But here's the thing, humans aren't machines. Not everyone's cut out for the traditional 9-5 grind. Our nature, rhythm, personality, and skills cannot fit in the same box. For some people, working a 9-5 is their ticket to success, but for others, it stifles their talents and strengths.

Some people are lucky enough to have incredible 9-5 jobs that they're passionate about, that are purpose driven and leave an impact, while others just see it as a paycheck.

So, if you're one of those who actually enjoy their 9-5, then that's great, you've hit the jackpot! But trust me, this chapter of the book will still help widen your mind to new ways of thinking that will benefit you in your job role.

Before we get into this chapter, I just want to let you know that this chapter will NOT tell you to quit your job or try to sell you on the idea of being an entrepreneur, like many other "self-help" jargons do.

Why? Because I don't think being an entrepreneur is for everyone and in today's society, especially on social media, it's been glamorized far too much. Not everyone wants to be their own boss, and that's perfectly fine.

So, don't skip this chapter just yet. Trust me, there are some golden gems in here that might just change your perspective. And I mean, you've already made it this far, so why not keep reading? These next few pages might be exactly what you need.

Now, you might be wondering, just what is this chapter even about?

Well, it's about the lack of choice we've been given when it comes to our careers.

It's about how we've been brainwashed from a young age to follow this one path.

This one path of traditional schooling, college, and university, all in the pursuit of becoming obedient workers.

And let's be real, sadly the majority who work 9-5s despise their jobs and are dragging themselves through another day to make it to the weekend or their next vacation day.

This path that society has laid out for us is the only one we're taught to see as "success" so we "should" follow it. But it's blindly following others that keeps us trapped in the rat race.

So, don't you think you deserve the freedom to CHOOSE your own version of success, instead of settling for society's narrow-minded definition?

Well, that's exactly what this chapter is about.

This constant pressure to succeed in the eyes of the world is one of the factors causing us major stress. It's keeping us so busy chasing after "success" that we don't even have the time or energy to think about what it really means to be successful and, most importantly, happy.

The more you're stuck in survival mode by doing what you think you "should" be doing, the more you get trapped in this cycle of rat race.

But the reality is that you can carve your own path. You don't have to follow the traditional path of what success means to others, but instead recreate what being successful is to your soul and purpose.

You might be thinking, hey Yas, that's easier said than done. Trust me, I know. But let me share a little bit of my story.

When I started out, I did things the traditional way. I went to a Church of England High School (that was run by nuns back in the day), got "good grades", stayed out of trouble, kept in line, and went to university to study a Bachelor of Science in Psychology.

While in university, I worked part-time at a luxury clothing store as a Sales Advisor.

After graduating, I pursued professional training and became a school counselor. But that was the year I hit rock bottom (as mentioned in the previous chapter), and I realized the conventional route wasn't working for me.

I did everything that I was "supposed" to do but I wasn't happy.

And so, I was forced to change things.

This is when I stumbled upon a whole new side of Psychology that I never knew existed. I dived into studying and training in Clinical Hypnotherapy, Psychotherapy, Neuro-Linguistic Programming (NLP), Thetahealing, Energy healing, Chakra Balancing, and various other "unconventional" healing approaches, instead of just sticking to the traditional psychological methods.

Since then, I've been working on different projects, freelancing, and doing private 1:1 sessions with my clients. I was so happy with this decision to build my own brand and business instead of going through the traditional route… well, I thought I was.

I mean, I get to do what I love: learn, build an online community, have the freedom of time, the freedom to choose the projects I work on, and be my own boss.

But here's the thing. Even though I was doing great, a part of me deep inside still felt unworthy and ashamed. No matter how much I achieved in this path that I took, it never seemed enough.

It didn't give me the same boost as a new title or external validation from a 9-5 job.

I desperately wanted to prove myself as "successful" in the eyes of society and my parents. So, if anyone asked me, "What did you do today?" I would instantly feel triggered, get defensive, and anxiously overshare everything that I did to prove that I was "productive" with my day.

Over time, this was getting out of hand as I never allowed myself to take a break or relax because I didn't believe I deserved it. I kept telling myself I wasn't "worthy" of rest like the others who are working 9-5s.

But here's the crazy part: I was actually working more hours than those 9-5 jobs (as anyone who has a business knows) but because I was so programmed with success only being tied to a 9-5 job, I couldn't allow myself to see that I was successful. At least, not in the way school had conditioned me to be.

YOUR JOB DOES NOT DEFINE YOUR WORTH.

Throughout all of this, I never realized how much importance I placed on my job for my own self-worth. That is, until I met my husband who opened my eyes to the fact that a 9-5 job doesn't define a person's worth. He made me see that I had glamorized the idea of a 9-5 job in my mind.

It's scary to think that many of us spend 80% of our lives counting down the days until the weekend or our next vacation. Our most valuable asset is our time... so don't you think we must treat it with some significance and value?

In James Altucher's book, Skip the Line, there was a study that revealed something quite astonishing: people in 9-5 jobs only work an average of 2.5 hours a day. Yes, out of the 8 hours spent in their offices, **only 2.5 hours are actually productive**.

This finding is supported by more research that shows the average US worker is only productive for 2 hours and 53 minutes during an 8-hour workday.

The study also found that the top unproductive activities in the office include:

- Reading news websites – 1 hour and 5 minutes
- Social media – 44 minutes

- Discussing non-work-related topics – 40 minutes

- Searching for new jobs – 26 minutes

On top of that, the average office worker is interrupted every 3 minutes, and it takes them 23 minutes to get back on track after each interruption. It's no wonder, then, that productivity is so low with all these distractions.

These findings were a game-changer for me. Why? Because I realized that having a focused 2 hours of work is better than having 8 hours of constant distractions.

Why am I sharing this with you? Because most of us (including myself) have put the 9-5 job on a pedestal, thinking it's the key to feeling "successful".

From a young age, one of the first things we're asked is what we want to be when we grow up. But why aren't we asked other questions like who we want to become? Or what adventures we want to experience?

Why does the education system solely focus on careers rather than personal growth? Why has it conditioned children to think about what type of career they want instead of thinking about what type of people they want to become?

Imagine if schools taught children about successful habits and characteristics. How different would everything be?

Instead, we were taught that the only way to get ahead is to work harder than anyone else, take on more than we can handle, and then we'll be rewarded…maybe. Sometimes.

The problem with this mindset is that I've seen people who work themselves to the bone, yet struggle financially and never find true success and happiness. If hard work alone brought money and success, then nurses, teachers, farmers, garbage collectors, and those in the food service industry and fast food joints would be billionaires by now.

So, maybe, just maybe, success and wealth aren't solely determined by how hard we work, contrary to what we were taught in school. It's more of a mindset game, something schools purposely neglected to teach us.

THE RAT RACE

Let's take a quick look at the Oxford dictionary definition of the Rat Race:

A way of life in which people are caught up in a fiercely competitive struggle for wealth or power.

And the Cambridge Business English dictionary defines it as:

A way of life in modern society in which people compete with each other for power and money.

The animation below portrays it perfectly:

www.polyp.org.uk
animated version- www.foei.org/livemore

"The trouble with the rat race is that even if you win, you're still a rat," – Lily Tomlin

The rat race isn't just about the typical 9-5 grind. It's the reason we're all so consumed with consumerism, competition, and this scarcity mindset.

This system brainwashes us into thinking that true happiness comes from being a part of the system, getting that promotion, or owning the latest iPhone.

But that is not true.

For years, we've been tricked into thinking that working ourselves to the bone, barely making ends meet, and numbing our souls with things that we know aren't good for us is normal. Whether it's stuffing our faces with fast food, drowning our sorrows in drugs and alcohol, or mindlessly scrolling through social media for hours on end. The rat race has made us believe that hating Mondays and being perpetually exhausted is just a normal part of life. It has made us normalize being so tired that when the weekend comes, most of us are so drained that we end up doing everything we can to let loose and burn off steam.

Or just sleep all day.

SO, WHAT'S WRONG WITH THE RAT RACE?

"If they used the power of the mirror, they would have asked themselves, "Does this make sense?" All too often, instead of trusting their inner wisdom, that genius inside, most people follow the crowd. They do things because everybody else does them. They conform, rather than question," – Rich Dad Poor Dad

Well, as we have covered above, the rat race rides on the foundational belief that we must work hard in order to consume more, so we can feel "good enough" or find that happiness we so desperately crave.

It thrives on our desperate desire for happiness and success.

It knows we'll do whatever it takes to achieve it.

So, it keeps pushing us to want **more**, promising that happiness is just around the corner.

There's a great saying by James Altucher that resonates with this perfectly:

"The learned man aims for more. But the wise man decreases. And then decreases again."

What does this mean?

Let's think about it. We live in a world where we always want bigger, better, and more. Two cars instead of one, a bigger house, a bigger TV, the latest gadgets, and so on. Our standard of living keeps skyrocketing without us even realizing it.

Take the latest iPhone 14 Pro, for example. People were literally standing in line for hours just to get their hands on one. And guess what? Most of them don't even need a new phone! But they want it anyway because, well, everyone else has it.

But you know what's even crazier? Many of these people don't even have the funds or extra money for it! They know that buying this phone will put them in some financial stress, but they do it anyway.

Why do you think this happens?

Well, it's all about "keeping up with the Joneses." This phrase has been around since 1913, originating from a comic strip by Arthur R that showed a family trying to keep up with their neighbors, the Joneses. This concept illustrates how society judges us based on our material possessions and lifestyle, which in turn we tie our worth to.

Here's the thing. If we keep living with this mindset, we'll never be satisfied. No matter how much stuff we accumulate, there will always be someone with more. So, we'll always feel like we need more. It's a never-ending cycle.

And isn't it a strange coincidence that there's a show called "Keeping Up With the Kardashians" that perfectly embodies this idea? Just a little food for thought.

HOW DOES THIS AFFECT US?

Well, the social effects of this concept is that people are influenced to want to fit in and conform to what the majority thinks is cool.

Take TikTok, for example. When there's a popular trend or dance, everyone jumps on board and follows along.

It's just human nature to want to be accepted and "fit in" with society.

But why are we so obsessed with fitting in, you ask?

Well, it goes way back to our ancestors and their survival instincts. Back in the day, they lived in tribes, and being part of the tribe meant you had access to food, water, and shelter. To stay in the tribe, you had to play by their rules and "norms". If you didn't, you'd get kicked out and left to fend for yourself in the wild. Not a great situation, right?

An article of Psychology Today titled "We All Want to Fit In" by Lybia Ma explains this further; here's an excerpt of it:

"How much time should your kids spend online?

Ten cool things you should be watching on Netflix

Clothes you shouldn't wear after fifty

These are real headlines, telling us what we should be reading, watching, wearing and thinking. Magazines and newspapers are filled with shoulds and should nots, musts and must nots. But we don't read these articles to find out how much time our children should be spending on the internet, or even what we should be wearing in any given situation. We read them to make sure we're doing the same as everyone else. We read them to make sure we fit in.

...or the playground, we first begin to notice the differences between ourselves and other children, and we start to mirror the behavior of a dominant group in order to be accepted by them. This mimicry continues into adulthood...if we're doing the same as everyone else, we must be doing it right, and finding a reflection of ourselves in those around us is a form of validation."

In my opinion, it's this **need to fit in** that drives us toward materialism and consumerism. We want to have the same type of games, shoes, bags, phones, cars, and clothes that the rich and famous have, so we can feel equal and "worthy". We want to have the same stuff as the "dominant" group in the playground that is society, AKA those who have a seat on the popular table.

To be more specific, there's this term called "conspicuous consumption" where you spend money on luxury items to show off how "rich" you are. If you don't have the latest car, designer bad, or go to a wait-listed luxury restaurant that everyone is "dying" to go to, then you're basically an outcast.

And you know those midlife crises people talk about? Yeah, they're not normal. Why do people in their 40s or 50s suddenly start self-sabotaging their lives? Cheating, losing jobs, wasting money on gambled investments, drinking alcohol like fish?

Why sacrifice the incredible years you still have left? The average person lives up to 90. Half of your life isn't even lived yet. Don't sacrifice your today for some imaginary future with a "retirement fund". You still have so much life to live.

THE FRIDGE STORY

Years ago, back when we lived in our house in England, I remember we had a fridge.

Just a regular, average-sized fridge. Nothing fancy.

We never really thought much about its size until one day, my dad surprised us with a new, much bigger fridge. Before we knew it, without even realizing it, we started buying more groceries and snacks to fill up this new fridge.

But soon enough, even the bigger fridge couldn't fit all our food anymore.

Strange.

We couldn't even fathom how we managed with the older, smaller fridge without any complaints.

Then, as weeks went by, I remember visiting my friend's house and noticed they had the fridge that made ice and had coolers outside of it. And then a few weeks after that, I visited another friend who had a fridge with a touch screen. A TOUCH SCREEN.

And that's when it hit me: there will always be something greater, bigger, or more luxurious than what we already have. Whether it's a bigger TV, the latest iPhone, a fancier car, or the newest designer bag. It's never-ending.

And if we keep chasing after these things, NOTHING will ever be enough.

The catch is that we are already enough just as we are, without all the extra fluff that consumer culture makes us think we need. It's like when you buy a bigger fridge and end up spending more on groceries to fill it up. The same goes for buying a bigger house – most people end up buying more furniture for it, spending way more than they planned.

Now, let's think about this logically for a moment.

Do you honestly believe that making more money, driving a bigger car, having a bigger house, or owning more things will make you happier?

It seems like many people focus so much on these material possessions, wasting both their time and energy on them, that they forget about the more important things in life: friends, family, meaning, and fun.

And that's not really living.

In James Altucher's book, Choose Yourself, he found that:

"Credit card debt went from $700 billion in 2005 to $2.5 TRILLION in 2007. Two short years. Now everybody has wide screen TVs, two houses, the latest Viking kitchen equipment, a boat, two environmentally sustainable cars (to assuage the guilt for their voracious consumption), and ate out two or three times a week."

Our level of consumption has increased dramatically over the years, and now with social media, we're constantly comparing our lifestyles and feeling the pressure to keep up. It's toxic and it won't ever lead to true happiness. Don't fall into this trap.

HOW TO BREAK FREE

1. Reject the Joneses

"If you live for having it all, what you have is never enough," – Vicki Robin

This obsession with always having the biggest, the best, and the flashiest things is not something we can maintain.

There will always be someone out there who appears to be younger, happier, or more successful than you.

You can never win this never-ending race.

Instead, focus on the things that bring you real joy. Now, I'm not asking you to never buy new things, but just don't mindlessly consume things because you think it will make you feel a certain way or "look great" in the eyes of society. Pause and ask yourself before buying, do YOU, the real authentic you inside, really want this thing?

There's a book called The Having by Suh Yoon Lee that uses a great technique for this called "having signals". This is about how we have inner "signals" when we buy things and show us whether we really want a certain thing or not. Deep down, we know whether this is a good purchase or a bad purchase. A purchase fueled by the wrong reasons often makes you feel guilty and heavy afterward, not excited or joyful.

2. Realize Your Power

You don't need external validation to feel powerful.

Society wants to keep you trapped in this rat race, all safe and comfortable, by taking away your power. But how can you truly spread your wings and soar when you're stuck in a cage?

In the book Choose Yourself by James Altucher, it says:

"Human beings are born pioneers. The rise of corporatism (as opposed to capitalism) forced people into cubicles instead of out into the world, exploring and inventing and manifesting."

As we talked about in the previous chapter about traditional schooling, we are all born a GENIUS. It's the system that knocks it out of us.

But you know what? You can choose yourself.

You can believe in your own potential to achieve the so-called "impossible".

We live in a world now where success is no longer about waiting to be "chosen" by someone else. You define what success means to you. Want to be an author? Self-publish that book. Want to be a director? Make your own movie and share it with the world on social media. The possibilities are endless. You don't have to wait for any form of "stamped approval" to reach the goals that you want.

3. Create Urgency

Society gives us just two days to escape from our mundane life. The rest of the week, the five days, are spent in this comfortable mediocrity. And comfort breeds complacency. That's why most people don't make a change until they hit rock bottom.

So, let's create some urgency. Imagine you're in prison, and the only way out is to start a successful business. You would do whatever it takes to make that happen, right?

Well, life shouldn't have to push you to the brink before you make a change.

Don't wait until you're bankrupt to start making the necessary changes.

Take control of your life *now*.

4. Build Your Own Brand

Trust me, I was the last one to jump onto social media when it came out.

I mean, I only caved and made a Facebook account back in high school because I didn't want to feel left out. But honestly, I hardly used it.

Years later, I strongly resisted creating an Instagram account. It took one of my university friends creating an account for me called "olives and cheese" (which were two of my favorite things at the time, until I found out I was lactose intolerant. Whoops.) before I even considered joining that platform.

But once I graduated university and started working, I realized just how powerful building and having an online community can be. Especially during some of the darkest periods of my life.

Social media became a way for me to share my journey, my struggles, and all the lessons I was learning along the way. And guess what? That's actually why you're holding this book right now.

During one of my roughest patches, I was gratefully able to build an Instagram community called **Inspire with Yas**, and let me tell you, it opened up so many doors for me. I connected with some truly incredible people and ended up with some amazing opportunities. Like being a co-partner on an online course, speaking at many events, getting many of my clients, being a part of a panel, being a speaker at an International Psychology Conference, and even getting featured in media outlets and blogs. It's been quite the ride.

This is why whether it's social media, a website, a blog, a newsletter, or an email list, you have to start building your online presence. Seriously, in today's world, if you're not online, it's like you don't exist. No joke.

So, even if you're content with your 9-5 job, you should still create your online community on platforms like Instagram, YouTube, TikTok, LinkedIn, Facebook, Twitter, and so on. Having an online presence or a personal brand can do wonders for you, trust me. It opens up opportunities you never even dreamed of.

I mean, look at it this way, online means GLOBAL. Collaborating requests, speaking, writing, art, and music projects, better job offers – you name it, it's possible. And the best part? It doesn't have to be related to your job or anything.

Maybe you have a deep interest in fishing, for example. Then you can share your experiences, post funny fishing memes, talk about the best fishing gear – you get the idea.

Your interests could be true crime, cats, health and wellness, nutrition, mental health, psychology, finance, conspiracy theories, journalism, politics, fantasy books, candles, music, anything. You don't need to be an expert in a specific area or topic to build your personal brand. You can even be a master of nothing and simply talk about your day, share jokes or lessons that could benefit others.

Your personal brand can become a hobby, a side hustle, land you a massive deal, or even become a way to make passive income. I mean, there's this girl on TikTok who landed a six-figure publishing deal just by sharing her book idea on her page after being rejected by other publishers. Talk about unexpected success, right?

The point is, you never know what could happen for you.

So, whether you're stuck in the 9-5 grind or not, building your own platform is your ticket out of the rat race. It's your chance to create your own opportunities instead of waiting around for them to come to you. It's your way of defining success on your own terms.

So, go for it. The choice is yours.

5. Read More Success Stories

Seriously, keep reading them.

"That's impossible."

"No one was able to do that."

"Some people are just lucky."

If others did it, it means you can do it too.

Don't let other people's fear or limited views hold you back from the incredible possibilities that exist in this world.

There are people out there who have created miracles and are living their dream lives. I count myself among them, not because I'm lucky, but because I've put in the work and applied a lot of the tips that I'm sharing with you in this book. And hey, they're not just for you – they're a reminder for me too.

So, expose yourself to the people who have already achieved what you desire in life. It could be an amazing marriage or relationship, a thriving business, strong family bonds, solid friendships, unshakable confidence, or even the freedom of time to do what you love. Read about their journeys and soak up their wisdom. You don't have to know them personally.

I've been inspired by people I've never met, just by diving into their books and reading them over and over again. And the reason I stress the importance of rereading and immersing yourself in positive stories is to firmly plant in your mind that YES, IT IS **POSSIBLE**.

Surround yourself with those who embody what you aspire to be. Whether it's through books, real-life mentors, or even mentors you've never had the chance to meet.

Let their stories and guidance shape your own path.

CHAPTER 5

LIE #5: TALKING ABOUT MONEY IS TABOO

Hey there. Welcome to the first of the two money chapters in this book.

Can you believe this whole money thing is actually one of the biggest lies we've been fed to hold us back?

So, I'll be honest with you, these two money chapters were a real pain for me to write.

I mean, I procrastinated like crazy for months!

Every time I tried to sit down and get to business, I found myself…

- Going down a YouTube rabbit hole

- Watching the most random and hilarious videos my younger sister sends me

- Bombarding and re-sharing those videos to my husband

- Organizing my kitchen cupboard (for the 5th time that week)

- Deciding to reply back to all my 600 unopened emails

- Opening and closing the snack cupboard multiple times a day, staring blankly at it

- Opening and closing the fridge for no actual reason

- Grabbing snacks even though I wasn't hungry

- Deciding to do the laundry

- Sending random stupid selfies to both of my sisters

- Calling my parents for the 4th time that day, just to say hi

- Googling "how to stop procrastinating"

So, as you could tell, I was doing anything and everything EXCEPT ACTUALLY WRITING THIS DAMN CHAPTER.

It was a mess, I tell you.

But one day, I woke up and realized that if I wanted to finish this book, I had to confront my procrastination head on. So, I did what I always do when I'm feeling stuck – I turned to my trusty journal.

I poured out all my feelings I experienced whenever I simply opened the word document for this chapter. And then I realized that my imposter syndrome was taking control here. I mean, WHO WAS I to write about money? I'm no billionaire or the founder of some mega-corporation.

But here's the thing – I may not have billions in the bank, but I can definitely share how I healed my relationship with money and the psychology behind it. That's what truly changes your life and opens doors you never even knew existed.

My relationship with money now is a beautiful one. It's empowering, balanced, and healthy. I no longer feel ashamed or controlled by it. I've waved goodbye to all those fear-based scarcity-driven money beliefs that were passed down through generations in my family. The place where I am today required a lot of hard work. I started from scratch and had a lot of unlearning to do.

And that's why I believe that I'm fully equipped to share and help you heal your own relationship with money.

Can you imagine how liberating, how FREEING, it will feel when money no longer has a hold on you? When you realize that money has always had your back and that there's always enough to go around?

Trust me, it's a warm and fuzzy feeling that you'll experience after reading the next few pages.

But first... let's dive into the taboos and lies we were told about money.

"YOU SHOULDN'T SPEAK ABOUT MONEY"

Money is just as important to our well-being as our health and relationships. Like Zig Ziglar says, *"Money isn't the most important thing in life, but it's reasonably close to oxygen on the 'gotta have it' scale."*

But the funny thing is, our society and culture has a love/hate relationship when it comes to money. We're all taught to keep it hush hush, unlike other areas of our lives.

Think about it, if you walked into a room full of strangers and boldly announced, "I am totally committed to being as healthy as possible," what kind of reaction do you think you'd get?

Take a guess.

When I asked this question, the majority of the answers said that you'd get some respect, maybe even a round of applause and a couple of nods from the audience.

And if you switched it up and declared your dedication to having as much love in your life as possible, you'd probably get the ame response.

But now, picture this: you walk into the same room and proudly proclaim, "I am devoted to making or having as much money as possible!" What do you think would happen?

I bet most people would start making judgments about you as a person.

Selfish, materialistic, shallow, greedy – those are just a few of the lovely labels they might throw your way.

Some might even say you can't be spiritual and money-focused at the same time.

See what I mean?

Money is such a touchy subject that often brings shame and negativity. It's funny how people say, "Money isn't everything," but then spend most of their lives chasing after it.

I'm not saying money IS everything, but it's definitely a taboo topic that's rarely, if ever, discussed openly. Especially in certain households like Middle Eastern or Asian households.

Parents in those cultures usually feel this heavy responsibility to shield their children from financial struggles and never let them worry about money. But sweeping things under the rug or pretending they don't exist doesn't empower our children when it comes to money.

Kids are WAY smarter than we give them credit for, and they pick up on our energy and behaviors (by modeling) more than our words. If they see you freaking out about bills or getting into heated arguments with your partner over money, they start forming their own beliefs about money and the world. And all those beliefs get buried in our subconscious programming and are often not allowed to be opened or discussed.

It's like a vicious cycle – the more we hide our beliefs, the harder they are to work through.

So, by keeping conversations about money hidden and "taboo", we learn to not feel safe to even simply talk about it.

That's why we need to shine a light on our money beliefs and bring them out of darkness.

Because it's only when we shed light on the dark parts of ourselves that we can truly heal.

This reminds me of this story I have from when I was a school counselor.

I had this 7-year-old boy who kept having nightmares, so we worked on drawing out the "scary people" (as he called them) from his dreams and put them into paper in the daylight. I did my best to make it safe for him to confront his fears by looking at the "scary people" that he's just drawn, and guess what? The nightmares stopped.

Why? Because when we bring our fears into the daylight, they often don't seem so scary anymore.

It's simple, really.

Like when you're in a dark room and you think you see monsters, but then you turn on the light and realize it's just a pile of clothes.

Shedding light on our beliefs helps us become more self-aware and tackle what's holding us back. And you know what the first step to changing our beliefs is? Yes, you guessed it – awareness.

We can only become aware when we openly discuss money and money topics with the people we trust and feel close to.

So, let's start shining some light on our money beliefs and bring them out into the open.

HAPPY MONEY VS UNHAPPY MONEY

Happy money is when a kid uses their allowance to buy flowers for their mum on Mother's Day. It's when parents happily save a few extra bucks each week to send their kids to football camp or piano classes.

But it's not just about personal stuff. It's also about helping out struggling family members or sending some financial help to those affected by a hurricane. It's about investing in businesses or community projects. It's about getting paid for doing work that makes you and your clients happy.

Happy money is "happy" – it brings smiles and feelings of love and care.

On the other hand, unhappy money is paying rent, bills, or taxes. It's dealing with alimony after a nasty divorce. Or receiving a paycheck for a job you hate but can't leave. It's even buying the latest designer bag (that you know is overpriced) for the sole reason to feel "accepted" by your friends, not because you wanted it.

Unhappy money is "unhappy" in the sense that it brings frustration, anger, sadness, and despair.

It's not how much money you make or have, but the energy with which you give or receive it that determines your flow.

So, do you receive money with enthusiasm and gratitude?

According to Ken Honda, the author of Happy Money, *"Most people, whether they realize it or not, are already in a deeply committed, unhappy relationship with their money."*

And here's the thing: money does not magically come from "working harder".

We all know the obvious expenses like studying, loans, groceries, credit card debts, mortgage, and all that. But it often feels like there's never enough money left for what we're "supposed" to have. We're constantly bombarded with ads telling us we *need* the newest model of everything. We're made to feel like we're missing out if we don't keep up with our friends' extravagant trips and fancy purchases. There's even a whole term for this fear of missing out: FOMO.

Whether it's some fancy cosmetic cream or a new outfit that promises to make us look richer, more handsome or more beautiful, we're convinced that we have to buy it. It's this never-ending cycle of always needing something new. Advertisers, TV shows, and even our friends keep telling us that what we have isn't good enough anymore. And we tell ourselves that we're doing everything right, but it's never enough. Someone is always doing better or has something better.

So, we cry out, "It's not fair!"

But you know what? Many of us operate under the scarcity mindset. We believe that if someone else has something, then we can't have it. This mindset convinces us that there are limited resources in the world and if we don't get what we want, then someone else will.

In other words, we're driven by fear, jealousy, and greed.

Our parents play a big role in shaping our beliefs about money, but it's up to us to change these stories. We have unknowingly absorbed this scarcity mindset from our parents, but now it's time to break free and create a new story for ourselves.

A lot of people experience fear when it comes to money, which is an instinctive response.

If we don't pay close attention to our mindset, we may not even realize that fear is driving our actions, both at home and in our financial decisions.

The first step toward adopting a ZEN approach to money and our lives is through practicing gratitude. Instead of constantly feeling like there is never enough, we have to shift our thinking to appreciate all that we have and say, "I have all that I need, and I am grateful for it."

When money comes into our lives, we should express gratitude, and when it leaves us, we have to do the same. That is how we acknowledge the ways in which money has served us and remain grateful for it.

The second step is understanding that money involves being true to ourselves and sharing our unique abilities with the world. Negative emotions, such as anxiety, fear, doubt, guilt, and self-neglect, hinder our prosperity. Our minds can only process one emotion at a time, so we should shift our focus to abundance and positivity.

If our attitude toward our jobs and finances is negative, it will affect our overall life. Conversely, if our money blueprint is filled with happiness, joy, and a desire to help others, we will experience wealth in all aspects of our lives. But if our money blueprint is tainted with anger, hatred, and negative memories, our lives will also be filled with the same.

Define your own happiness.

Bhutan is known as one of the happiest nations in the world. Not everyone in Bhutan may appear outwardly happy, as many of them are shy and tend to hide when they encounter foreigners. But their happiness is more of a quiet contentment with everyday life and being satisfied with what they have. They have fewer worries due to a free healthcare system and the assurance that their friends or even the kind will support them in times of need.

HOW TO BREAK FREE

1. **Communicate.**

   Don't be afraid to share your thoughts about money with your family and loved ones.

   Ask your parents questions, and if you have children, keep an open and transparent channel of communication with them. Trust me, kids are way smarter than we give them credit for. Share and explain things to them too.

   Plus, I believe that children are sources of unfiltered raw wisdom in the purest unconditional loving form. So, you never know what even you might learn from them.

2. **Unlearn.**

   Take a good look at your parents' money mindset. See if there's anything that needs fixing or upgrading. Then, observe your own behavior and see if it matches with that of your parents.

If you do notice a similar pattern, ask yourself: Does this pattern serve me? What can I change? How can I create a more honest channel of communication with myself when it comes to money?

It's time to make a change. Get real with yourself. Start a money journal. Assess, reflect, and make different moves.

3. **Gain Knowledge.**

Check out social media pages that talk about money positively. There are tons out there that are dedicated to helping you break free from money beliefs.

The best part? These resources actually encourage open discussions about money and the beliefs we have around it. And honestly, that's what we need more of.

But remember, it's not just about gathering knowledge. It's about putting that knowledge into action.

CHAPTER 6

LIE #6: MONEY IS THE ROOT OF ALL EVIL

"We are living out a script around money right now that quite often somebody wrote for us generations ago," – Brad Klontz, a financial psychologist.

According to Klontz, these "money scripts" are unconscious beliefs that shape how you think about money. And it's these patterns of thinking that can often drive your financial behaviors as you grow up.

I mean, think about it.

How many of these societal beliefs (or should I say, societal lies) about happiness and success have been drilled into our heads?

It's the same deal when it comes to money.

Many of us grew up seeing our parents with their own strong beliefs about money.

Take a moment to reflect on your own views about money...

Do you still think you'd be a decent human being if you had a lot of money?

What do you think people would think of you if you had a lot of money?

Are you worried that money would somehow corrupt you?

These are all important questions.

It's time to ditch those collected beliefs.

Break up with them, let them go, and start fresh.

It's time to rewrite your money story and define your own path.

Let's have a little recap about our brains as little kids: When we are between the age of 0 and 7, our brains act like sponges and soak up all sorts of beliefs. These beliefs then end up shaping how we see the world. It's because our brains are still in the Theta brain wave, which makes us believe everything we hear.

That's why, most of the time, we adopt our parents' or caregivers' views on money without even realizing it.

In the book called The Having by Suh Yoon Lee, she tells the story of her dad who grew up extremely poor and would often go to sleep hungry. Even after he became a successful engineer in South Korea, he just couldn't shake off his frugal habits. He was always living in fear that his money would disappear, so he saved every penny he could. He saved money, water, electricity – you name it. He saved so much that he forgot how to really live.

He even missed out on holidays abroad with friends, golf outings, and even his favorite fish dish because it was "too expensive".

It was then revealed how her father, after being diagnosed with cancer, refused to stay in a private ward where he could be more comfortable. Even during his final days. Instead, he chose to stay in a hospital dorm ward that was shared with many others.

Suh Yoon followed in her father's footsteps. As she got older, she became just as frugal. She would spend hours on her phone trying to get refunds for her receipts, clipped coupons like it was her job, and even made special trips to the supermarket just to get discounted meat.

Now, this story teaches us something important: we have to break the cycle of money habits that runs in our families.

It's not easy.

Our society doesn't make it any easier either.

When we're asked to unlearn something as adults or start from scratch in something new, our ego freaks out. It hates leaving that comfortable zone and goes into survival mode. It's like, "Why change? You're doing just fine as you are. Don't mess it up!"

But real change requires us to step out of our comfort zone. And that scares the heck out of our minds. Because our minds are wired to keep us alive, not necessarily happy. They will do anything to protect us.

On a recent podcast I was listening to the other day, the host was talking about how Tony Robbins holds workshops for millionaires and billionaires. Yes, you read that right. And when the podcaster got the chance to attend the same workshop, she saw how these super rich people came in with a beginner mindset, eager to learn and grow.

It blew the host's mind, and mine too!

You'd think a billionaire would have more of an "ego" and wouldn't really want to learn anything else… Well, guess not.

See, traditional schooling has taught us that learning stops after we graduate from university. But that's not true. Real learning happens AFTER graduation. It's a never-ending journey.

That's what separates the successful people from the ones who never quite reach their potential.

So, here's the deal. If these billionaires can set their egos aside and approach life like beginners, why can't we? Seriously, think about it.

Now, let's play a little game, shall we?

Take a look at these statements and if any of them ring "true" to you, just raise your hand and give a little nod to yourself if you're by yourself in a café or on the plane and you don't want to freak people out.

"Money is the root of all evil."

"My financial success depends on the job market and the economy."

"God only likes the poor."

"Money doesn't grow on trees."

"Most wealthy people are selfish or greedy."

"You can't be spiritual and rich."

"It takes money to make money."

"The rich get richer and the poor get poorer."

"In order to climb the ladder of success, you have to step on others on the way up."

"No one can live a balanced, happy, and healthy life if they want to make money."

"It's lonely at the top."

"It's a dog-eat-dog world."

"Only a few writers, artists, actors, or musicians ever make money."

"There are only starving artists."

I could go on and on with this list, but you get my point.

Now, there's a crucial element of the law of attraction (like attracts like) that I would like to bring up here. We really do become magnets to the things that we believe to be true. If you have a certain belief, your mind will do everything in its power to make it true. The universe will bring you examples or put you in experiences that prove your beliefs to be true.

For example, if you believe that all rich people are selfish or greedy, you'll probably find yourself surrounded by those types. And that might lead to a lot of resentment too.

Or if you believe it's a dog-eat-dog world, you'll attract competitive co-workers who will step on you at every chance they get. It can feel like opportunities are limited.

And if you believe that you can't live a balanced, happy, and healthy life if you want to make money, well, you might end up sacrificing other things like your love life or your health. Eventually, your belief comes true.

The problem is, many of us unconsciously attract things we don't want because we focus on them. We attract things because we speak about what we DON'T want.

It's actually pretty simple, as demonstrated in the book "Money and the Law of Attraction" by Esther Hicks. The more you talk about what you don't want, the more it comes your way. Because speaking about it makes you a magnet for it, even if you don't actually want it.

Our minds don't really understand negatives.

For example, when you say "I don't want to be poor", your mind only registers it as "I want to be poor – it doesn't understand the "don't".

This is, I think, especially true when it comes to money, or the lack thereof.

So, if you keep talking about how there isn't enough money, or how everything is getting so expensive, or how there are no opportunities or affordable real estate, well, guess what? Your world starts reflecting those beliefs. It becomes your reality.

Also, don't you think it's interesting how mainstream movies and TV shows also shape our negative beliefs about money?

Have you ever noticed how they always portray "rich" people as cold, selfish, or evil?

And it's not just the entertainment industry, the mainstream media and news are also guilty of perpetuating this destructive cycle of thinking. They constantly bombard us with stories of war, disease, poverty, the crashing economy, or financial markets reaching an "all time low" on all their outlets. It's fear, fear, fear all the time.

Can you imagine how damaging this is to our beliefs about money? It affects our growth and quality of life in general, too.

But it makes sense, doesn't it? The mainstream media is just a bigger system that wants to control us. They don't want us to think for ourselves or realize our true inner power.

It's just like our outdated schooling system that trains us to be uncreative and unthinking.

In the book Outwitting the Devil by Napoleon Hill (that was written in 1938 but only allowed to be published to the public in recent years due to its "unconventional" title), he talks about how a person who **thinks** is a person who is dangerous to the devil. Dangerous to society.

Why? Because society doesn't like independent thinkers because they question things and don't blindly follow the norms and rules. They create their own rule book for life, rooted in FAITH instead of FEAR.

Independent thinkers believe in themselves and the process. They know that failure is just a stepping stone to success. They protect their minds from distractions and believe in the abundance of the universe. They understand that abundance is our birth right, but our own limitations and societal beliefs hold us back from receiving it.

In "The Having" by Suh Yoon Lee (one of my favorite books), there's a quote that perfectly describes abundance: *"Abundance is like sunshine, some people turn their backs to it, but it's always there, always shining."*

As Dave Ramsey says, financial behavior is 80% psychology. It's all about mindset.

"The single most powerful asset we all have is our mind. If it is trained well, it can create enormous wealth seemingly instantaneously. An untrained mind can also create extreme poverty that can crush a family for generations," – Robert Kiyosaki, Rich Dad Poor Dad

Now, let's get one thing straight:

YOUR WORDS MATTER. PAY ATTENTION.

If you keep saying things like "I'll never be rich" or "I'll never be able to afford that," guess what? You're going to make it happen. That prophecy will come true.

As much as it might sound "woo woo" to you, the way we talk shapes our reality.

That's why it's so important to change how you talk about yourself when it comes to money.

In the book Rich Dad Poor Dad, Robert talks about this idea wonderfully. Here's the excerpt:

"My rich dad, on the other hand, always referred to himself as rich. He would say things like, "I'm a rich man, and rich people don't do this." Even when he was flat broke after a major financial setback, he continued to refer to himself as a rich man. He would

cover himself by saying, "There is a difference between being poor and being broke. **Broke is temporary. Poor is eternal.**

For example, one dad had a habit of saying, "I can't afford it." The other dad forbade those words to be used. He insisted I ask, "How can I afford it?" One is a statement, and the other is a question. One lets you off the hook, and the other forces you to think."

According to Robert Kiyosaki, when you say you "can't afford something", your brain shuts down and gets lazy. But when you ask yourself, "how can I afford it?" your brain starts thinking in new ways and gets creative.

This mental workout can actually lead to more wealth.

At the end of the day, money is like energy. It's attracted to people who greet it with love and gratitude, not hate, fear, or anxiety. I mean, would YOU be attracted to something or someone who's always complaining, being negative, and living in fear? That every time you're near them, they reject you? No? Didn't think so. So, why would money be attracted to you if you have that kind of energy?

HOW TO BREAK FREE

1. Tell Yourself the Money Story You DO Want.

Picture this: imagine money just flowing to you effortlessly. It's attracted to you, loves you, and it's always showing up for you, no matter what.

Now, start telling yourself this story and really feel the emotions of gratitude of already living this kind of life.

It's not just the words you say that the universe responds to, but it's the emotions and feelings behind them. As the author Neville Goddard explains in his book titled "Feeling is the Secret". Instead of focusing on what you don't want in terms of money, shift your thoughts to what you do want.

If you keep thinking about the lack of money in your life or in society in general, guess what? You'll just keep attracting more of that lack. It's a law of nature. Every thought that you have carries a certain frequency, and thoughts of "lack" have a pretty low vibration. And you know what that means? Yes, more of those low-vibe thoughts coming your way.

So, next time you catch yourself complaining about the lack of money, or any negative money experience for that matter, ask yourself, "Well, now I know what I DON'T want. So, what DO I want?"

Think of these negative thoughts like pulling on a loose thread in your favorite sweater. If you keep pulling, you'll end up ruining the whole thing.

This is a technique that I learned from Abraham Hicks in their book 'Money and Law of Attraction' and it's seriously great. It helps you focus on more feel-good thoughts.

The story that you tell yourself is what you will experience, so choose your story carefully.

2. Be Cautious of Mainstream Media.

OK, let's talk about mainstream media. We mentioned earlier on in the chapter that this mainstream media doesn't really help when it comes to getting out of your negative thinking spiral.

I mean, sure, terrible stuff is happening in the world and we shouldn't be ignorant about it. But maybe, just maybe, it's time to fill our minds with more empowering news like new discoveries, life-changing inventions, or stories of amazing people.

Also, how can WE help those in need and create the change we desire in the world if we aren't acting in our highest potential? We need to be empowered to then empower others.

HOT TIP: I changed my default browser to one that shows me "daily good news that inspires". So, whenever I open Google, I'm greeted with positive news and inspirational quotes instead of the usual downer news from MSN or BBC. Trust me, it makes a big difference in my mood and productivity as soon as I open my laptop.

Also, try to focus on the opportunities that come with financial or market crashes. I know, it's not easy to shift your thoughts in that direction. But hey, this is where many people actually thrive. You can thrive in any kind of economy as long as you equip yourself with that unshakable abundant mindset.

3. Be Conscious of Your Environment.

Being around people who constantly complain about their lack of money, love, or opportunities drastically affects your ability to make positive changes and attract better thoughts.

A lot of the people around us have this victim mindset that they have made into their entire personality. And they don't even realize it half the time. But remember what we talked about in Chapter 2? There might be some secondary benefits that they're getting from that victim mentality. (You can go back and read the chapter if you need a refresher on those benefits.)

Look, I get it. Being in victim mode can be super comfortable. It's so easy to blame everything on your boss, the government, your partner, your kids, or the economy. But that's not going to help you reach your full potential.

Just remember, the people you choose to spend time with can either push you toward attracting abundance and becoming the person you're destined to be, or they can completely derail you and bring you down.

So, choose wisely.

There is a famous saying that money is attracted to movement. So, if you're in a negative environment that holds you back, how will you attain any movement?

4. Use Affirmations.

Affirmations are a game-changer when you need to shift your thoughts quickly.

Here are some examples of affirmations that aren't too "unbelievable":

- **The universe is full of abundance and opportunities.**
- **Everything is always working in my favor and prosperity.**
- **I am the creator of my own experiences.**
- **All prosperity begins with one simple belief that I CAN.**
- **Positive thoughts attract wealth effortlessly.**
- **The better I tell the story of abundance, the better I feel.**
- **Money is energy and will appear as I truly feel about it.**
- **I am getting better and better every day at managing my money.**

- **The more positive thoughts I have, the more effortlessly money can flow into my life.**

- **I am happy to understand that my thoughts have a direct influence over attracting money.**

- **I feel calm knowing that the only work I have to do is align my thoughts with positive ones about money.**

These affirmations are down to earth and relatable, unlike others that are too "out there" like:

- *I am a millionaire.*

- *I have billions of dollars in my bank account.*

- *I own an 8-bedroom beach house in LA and Hawaii.*

- *I own 3 Ferraris.*

- *I am made of gold.*

This use of unrealistic statements shown above is the reason, I believe, why affirmations don't work. Because simply stating something does not mean that our mind will automatically accept it as the truth.

Our minds are not stupid. When something is far from our current reality, it will be rejected. This only makes ourselves feel worse because on a vibrational level, we are nowhere near what we are saying.

It's all about gradually working your way up with affirmations that you truly believe in. Focus on the positive ones and the rest will fall into place.

5. Break Up With the "I Can't Afford it" or "I'm so Broke" Mindset.

Oh my, the countless times I've heard this sentence "I can't afford it" being thrown around is insane.

Trust me, it was once a part of my daily vocabulary too, until I realized how much these phrases hold us back. And I completely understand how much of an unconscious damaging habit it can become.

"I can't afford" is such a destructive statement, really. It's time to switch to more empowering alternatives.

Instead, ask yourself:

How can I afford it?

This question opens up your mind to new, creative possibilities.

Or use these phrases instead:

- **It's not in my budget.**

    Instead of blaming money, this statement acknowledges that it's not a priority at the moment and you can plan for it in the future. Which brings us to…

- **It's not a priority.**

    This powerful statement helps you realize that you have other things you value more at the moment.

6. **Replace "OR" with "AND".**

You don't have to choose between being a good person *or* a wealthy person.

You don't have to choose between being spiritual *or* acquiring wealth.

You don't have to choose between having a fulfilled love life *or* a wealthy life.

You can be a good person **AND** a wealthy person.

You can be spiritual **AND** have an abundance of money flowing to you effortlessly.

You can have money **AND** be with the love of your life.

You can be wealthy **AND** so much more.

Don't limit yourself with the word "or".

You are multifaceted and have magnificent layers with unlimited potential within you.

Think of yourself as the vast ocean or the boundless sky, where there are no limits.

7. **Money Magnifies You.**

Remember, money doesn't change you.

It magnifies who you already are.

Society often says that money will change us, but please don't buy into that. I've heard that so many times, even from those closest to me. But it's not true. I believe that money simply magnifies our true nature.

If you're a good person with good intentions, money will magnify and enhance that. Similarly, if you're a bad person with bad intentions, money will magnify and expand that.

Don't be so afraid of money. Stop giving it too much power. It's a neutral energy without any "evil" attached to it. It goes where you want it to go, where you will it to go. It's under your control, not the other way around.

8. It's Never Too Late to Rewrite Your Script.

In the book, Magic of Thinking Big, David Schwartz talks about failure thinking vs success thinking: *"Stop thinking I should have started years ago."* Dwelling on past regrets or thinking that you should have started earlier – that's failure thinking. Successful people don't think that way. Instead, think *"I'm going to start now, my best years are ahead of me."*

Just focus on starting now.

You have the power to change your money beliefs and improve your financial situation.

While money beliefs can be and are passed on from one generation to another, they do not have to be permanent.

Once you have identified your thinking patterns about money, it's time to examine how to change those beliefs.

Let go of the scarcity mindset and embrace abundance with mindful, deliberate steps toward your desired reality.

CHAPTER 7

LIE #7: YOUR WORTH IS BASED ON SOMETHING EXTERNAL

I've always felt a void inside me. This deep void where I never felt good enough. Good enough to live the life I dream of, to have the money I desire, to be accepted for who I truly am, and even to feel confident in my own skin.

It was frustrating because I tried everything to fill that void. I worked hard to improve my appearance – losing weight, achieving a clear skin, having the healthiest hair, and dressing in the nicest clothes. But no matter how much I changed on the outside, it didn't change how I felt on the inside.

That feeling of heaviness and self-loathing would still creep in whenever I looked at myself in the mirror.

I fell into the trap of believing in the promises of beauty products. I chased any new skin and hair care products that "guaranteed" to make me look beautiful, all so I could finally feel "good enough". I spent hours researching and buying countless vitamins that also "guaranteed" to make me feel beautiful and confident. But no matter how much I invested in these products, they never made a difference in how I truly felt about myself.

Isn't it crazy how much we buy into the idea of "feeling and looking great" based on advertising? Especially when it comes to the things marketed for women to look younger, thinner, and more beautiful? We are bombarded with messages telling us that if we have the right perfume, flawless skin, or trendy clothes, we will feel desirable and respected.

Skin care and beauty are some of the biggest industries that prey on your insecurities. They will tell you that getting this glowing foundation and lipstick will finally make you beautiful. That getting this anti-aging cream will get you your life and your ex-husband back. That getting those shoes with this designer bag will finally make you feel seen and heard by others. They have made us crazy obsessive with our looks, with the idea of looking "flawless", in hopes that everything else in our lives will follow suit.

But the truth is, looking flawless and having all those things doesn't guarantee happiness or success. I recently read a book by Shonda Rhimes called the Year of Yes, where she shared her own experience with chasing perfection. As a teenager, she would spend hours trying to recreate Whitney Houston's "flawless" hair, only to find out years later that it was a WIG. A WIG. It was not real.

She had believed that if she had the perfect hair, then everything else in her life will be perfect too, but this changed everything for her. It was a wake-up call for her, realizing that her quest for flawless hair wasn't bringing her the fulfillment she thought it would.

It's disheartening to think about how much we're influenced by celebrities and social media. This chase for "flawless beauty" that Hollywood actresses and singers portray really affects our self-worth and self-esteem, especially when we're just growing up. Advertisers know this. They use famous faces to sell us their products. We're constantly trying to emulate their lifestyles, fashion choices, and even vacation destinations. And now, with the rise of social media "influencers", this pressure to conform and buy into trends is even more prevalent.

Just look at TikTok, where THE MOST TRENDING hashtag is "tiktokmademebuyit". What do you think that signifies?

It's crazy to think about how much power social media has over our purchases. We're constantly bombarded with people promoting products and convincing us that we need them to be happy and successful and beautiful and respected and whatnot.

But for me, no matter how many creams, treatments, or facials I tried from TikTok or other social media platforms, the void remained.

I would bend over backwards, sacrificing my boundaries and mental health, in a desperate attempt to please others, hoping that maybe getting their validation would fill this emptiness.

Sadly, it didn't.

No amount of compliments, weight loss, academic achievements, or personal accomplishments could fill that void. No matter how many books I read or how many training sessions I went to. No matter how many friends or networks I had.

No matter what I did or achieved, the emptiness was there to stay.

I believe that the feeling of "not being good enough" is an epidemic in today's society. Almost everyone has questioned their worth at some point. Majority of them have at least asked the question, "Why am I not good enough?"

It's true that insecurities and self-doubt are natural, but what happens when they consume your every thought and dictate your actions and emotions?

What happens when these insecurities start affecting your personal, romantic, social, or professional life?

Not feeling good enough can manifest itself through our daily actions and behaviors. How?

Well, do any of these sound familiar to you?

- You feel like a fraud or an imposter.
- You over-prepare just to impress others.
- You feel like you don't deserve your success.
- Even though you're doing a great job and due for a raise, you won't ask for it.
- You hold back from speaking up and avoid contributing because you think your thoughts aren't important.
- You procrastinate to avoid doing tasks that are challenging rather than risking the thought of "failure".
- Even though you're on the right track and doing well at work, you sabotage it.
- You feel like you're never really accepted or that you don't belong.
- You feel like an outsider looking in.

- You people please just to be loved and accepted by others.

- You allow your boundaries to be stepped on and struggle to say NO.

- You sabotage fulfilling and healthy relationships because you think you don't deserve them.

- You allow yourself to be taken advantage of or not be treated right because you think that's what you deserve.

- You automatically dismiss any form of success you achieve and attribute it to "luck" or just being in the right place at the right time.

- You believe that everyone is harshly evaluating you all the time.

Did any of these resonate with you? Did you nod your head twice, or maybe 45 times?

These were just a few examples of how "not feeling good enough" can impact your everyday life. But don't worry, you can become FREE from these. Trust me, I know because I was THE living embodiment of not feeling good enough. If I can overcome it, so can you.

I do believe that being originally from Egypt but growing up in the UK with my frizzy dark hair, chubby cheeks, and different skin color definitely did a number on my self-esteem. My different appearance played a massive role in my "not good enough" wound. I mean, I already felt like the odd one out compared to the other girls in my class. And let's face it, being labeled as "different" like we're often taught...isn't exactly a confidence booster, you know?

Now, the term "imposter syndrome" is closely tied to "not feeling good enough". It's a pattern of self-doubt, negative thoughts, and self-sabotage. A Psychology Today article by Janina Scarlet perfectly articulated it as *"it is almost like there is a monster sitting on your shoulder, whispering the worst things about you and making you doubt your every move."*

I believe that the rise in not feeling good enough and imposter syndrome, especially among women, is a result of the societal programming we've been subjected to about what it means to be "worthy".

A survey mentioned in a Forbes article revealed that women may experience imposter syndrome more than men. Why? Well, they attributed it to differences in how boys and girls are raised. Boys are encouraged to lead, be confident, and show less emotions from a young age. Women also face expectations from their families, gender roles, societal stereotypes, and cultural differences that contribute to self-doubt.

Additionally, self-imposed pressures and self-criticism play a significant role in fostering doubt and uncertainty.

"I have taught thousands of individuals and I see one thing in common in all of us, myself included. We all have tremendous potential, and we all are blessed with gifts. Yet the one thing that holds all of us back is some degree of self-doubt. It is not so much the lack of technical information that holds us back, but more the lack of self-confidence. Some are more affected than others.

Yet as a teacher, I recognized that it was excessive fear and self-doubt that were the greatest detractors of personal genius. It broke my heart to see students know the answers, yet lack the courage to act on the answer. Often in the real world, it's not the same smart people who get ahead, but the bold." – Robert Kiyosaki, Rich Dad Poor Dad

In our society, we are taught that our worth is determined by external factors. We are led to believe that our value lies in our work or job title, our relationship status, the car we drive, our academic achievements and diplomas, our family name, our appearance and looks, the clothes we wear, or our body size.

But SPOILER ALERT… none of these things actually define our worth.

They are all meaningless.

We have been conditioned to believe that in order to be considered "worthy", we must meet certain criteria and check off ALL the boxes. Only then are we granted access to the exclusive club of "worthiness". And only then, we believe, can we ask for that promotion, speak up in meetings, feel confident, have healthy relationships, receive love, attract our soulmate, experience happiness, or achieve success.

But you know what the truth is?

The truth is that you're already worthy just as you are. You were born into this world as a worthy individual. Whole and good enough. Just like every baby who enters this world.

Do you think they sit and stew, thinking about how they are unworthy? No, of course not. It's ridiculous to think about. They know they deserve love and expect it. And so should you.

Even young kids have this incredible ability to believe that they can achieve anything without questioning their own value or abilities. Ask a child what they want to be when they grow up, and you'll receive answers like:

"I want to be president."

"I want to be the queen of the world."

"I want to be an astronaut."

"I want to be a flying rocket."

"I want to be a princess."

"I want to be a superhero."

These are some of the answers I've personally received from kids.

Kids have an unlimited and expansive perception of themselves and the world. They believe that anything is possible and that they deserve it. They don't overthink or doubt their dreams for being "unrealistic". Nor do they doubt their skills or selves to achieve anything they want.

Now, let's consider this: if toddlers constantly doubted themselves, do you think they would ever learn how to walk or talk? Especially after their first fall or jumbled up word? Would they say, "well, walking just isn't for me"?

Of course not. It sounds ridiculous, doesn't it?

So, why do WE do this to ourselves as we grow older?

Remember, your worth and value remain constant, regardless of external factors. Let this chapter serve as a reminder whenever you need it. You are enough, just as you are. And to help you see things from a different perspective, here is a snippet of a life-changing motivational speech by Jeremy Anderson:

"Let me speak to that person that feels like they've lost their worth and their value.

This is a dollar bill. Now, if I go to the store and there's something for ninety cents, can I buy it with this dollar bill? OK, all right. So, if I go to the store and there's something for eighty five cents and after the tax it ends up being ninety six cents, can I buy it with this dollar bill? OK, all right.

So, what if I ball the dollar bill up? Think about it now. I just balled the dollar bill up, so it can't be worth a dollar now. It's probably worth like ninety five cents, right? How much do you think it's worth?

...I just balled it up, so clearly it's not worth a dollar anymore. All right. So maybe, what if I step on it? What if I stomped it? I just stomped it – how much is it worth now? Maybe sixty five cents, or sixty eight cents?

It's still worth a dollar?

OK, what if I ball it up, what if I step on it, and then I put it in the trash can; and it's in here with some trash, around some beer and some gum, and a bunch of the nasty stuff; and some guy off the street pulls the dollar out, unfolds it? How much is it worth now? Maybe eighty two cents? No? Come on, at least ninety two cents? OK.

So what if I ball up it, what if I step on it, what if I put it in trash, and then – watch this – I tear it in half? Think about it now. How much is it worth now?

A dollar? I can tape it?

Wait, wait, wait. Wait a second.

I just, I JUST balled it up, stepped on it, put it in trash, pulled it out, then I tore it in half, and you mean to tell me I could pick the dollar up, I could wipe it off, and I could put some tape around it, and it's still worth a dollar?

Then WHY, if this dollar doesn't lose its worth and value, then why do you feel like you've lost your worth and value?

Because many of you feel like you've been stepped on. You feel like you've been pushed aside. You feel like you've been abandoned. You feel like you've been abused. Like someone took from you.

Someone hurt you. Somebody took advantage of you. And deep down inside your core, you feel like you've lost some of your value.

...I'm here to tell you that you were created and you're born and you're here and you have life and you have purpose and you have value.

I am here to tell you that you still got worth and value and there's NOTHING that can happen that could take your worth and your value away."

Now, wasn't that beautiful?

Always remember that you're here on this planet because you bring value to the people around you. You're important, and the world needs you. People need you.

Embracing who you truly are and sharing that with the world is the most amazing thing you can do. And guess what? By being yourself, you inspire others to do the same.

In this book called "The Top Five Regrets of the Dying", Bronnie Ware, a nurse in Australia, documented the regrets of those nearing the end of their lives. The most common regret was *"I wish I had the courage to live a life true to myself, not the life others expected of me."*

This is a powerful reminder that we can't please everyone, and seeking validation from others doesn't determine our worth.

It reminds me of a folklore story that my mum used to tell us whenever we felt the need to "please everyone". It's about an old man, a young boy, and a donkey.

THE MAN, THE BOY, AND THE DONKEY

A man and his son were once going with their donkey to market. As they were walking along by his side a countryman passed them and said, "You fools, what is a donkey for but to ride upon?" So the man put the boy on the donkey, and they went on their way.

But soon they passed a group of men, one of whom said, "See that lazy youngster, he lets his father walk while he rides."

So the man ordered his boy to get off, and got on himself. But they hadn't gone far when they passed two women, one of whom said to the other, "Shame on that lazy lout to let his poor little son trudge along."

Well, the man didn't know what to do, but at last he took his boy up before him on the donkey. By this time, they had come to the town, and the passers-by began to jeer and point at them. The man stopped and asked what they were scoffing at.

The men said, "Aren't you ashamed of yourself for overloading that poor donkey of yours – you and your hulking son?"

The man and boy got off and tried to think what to do. They thought and they thought, until at last they cut down a pole, tied the donkey's feet to it, and raised the pole and the donkey to their shoulders. They went along amid the laughter of all who met them until they came to a bridge, when the donkey, getting one of his feet loose, kicked out and caused the boy to drop his end of the pole. In the struggle the donkey fell over the bridge, and his forefeet being tied together, he was drowned.

Try to please everyone, and you will please no one.

The moral of the story is to stop trying to impress people and chasing external validation. Instead, focus on impressing yourself. Push yourself, challenge yourself, and be the best version of you that you can be.

Because, here's the thing, no matter how you choose to live your life or the choices you make, there will always be someone who disagrees. Whether it's trying to please your parents or loved ones, in the end, you're the one who loses.

Trust me, I understand the pressure that Middle Eastern, Arab, and Asian households can put on us to make our parents happy. It becomes such a normal thing and we don't even question it, like it's a "duty".

But remember, while it's great to make them happy, it should NOT come at the cost of your own life, mental health, and happiness. Those should be your priorities before making others happy.

Building your self-worth starts by building your self-confidence in your decisions and choices, without constantly seeking external validation (especially from your parents or those closest to you). But before you can do that, you need to let go of this idea of being "perfect".

I've found that perfectionism is not actually a reflection of how hard you're working or how productive you are.

Perfectionism is a toxic mindset that sets unattainable standards, leading to constant self-criticism. It prevents you from feeling proud of yourself or truly celebrating your success. Plus, it can even lead to burnout.

Perfectionism often stems from childhood experiences, where your parents may have had unrealistic expectations or constantly compared you to others. And you never recognized it or broke free from those patterns.

A friend of mine once told me the crazy memories she had about her mum being extremely self-critical and harsh on herself. Apparently, whenever her mum made a mistake, even something as simple as taking the wrong turn, she would raise her hands and start banging her forehead while muttering "stupid stupid stupid" to herself.

Well, my friend later ended up picking up this same habit whenever she messed up, and she always felt this pressure to be "perfect".

Then, there's another friend of mine who grew up in a house where her parents were constantly arguing. Her dad would nitpick about the TINIEST things, like "not putting enough salt on the chicken" or "the food being cold" or "forgetting to take out the washing."

Can you imagine growing up in that kind of environment? It's like you're forced to believe that you have to be flawless in order to be loved or feel worthy. And if you do mess up, you better believe you're going to beat yourself up about it.

Now, let me tell you about my own cooking adventures.

When I got married and started cooking more often (shout out to my incredible mum who always took the time and effort to make us the best healthy family meals growing up), I realized that I would freak out over the smallest things. Burning the bottom of the rice, putting too much salt, not putting enough salt, over seasoning in general, leaving the cake for too long in the oven, forgetting to take out the chicken from the freezer on time, using too much baking soda in the cake (which made it taste disgusting), you name it. I'd beat myself up for hours, even days, over these little mistakes.

My reaction to these normal, everyday cooking mistakes was way too critical. And the crazy thing is, nobody else really cared!

We live in a culture that seems to have forgotten that we're all flawed. Yet, in that space is where our humanity lies. It's what makes us human.

I think we need to remind ourselves that we do not have a capacity for perfection – it doesn't exist. But our desire to do better is what makes it incredibly powerful.

Striving for perfectionism will only lead to burnout. It's so exhausting to constantly live in this state of fear and anxiety, never allowing yourself to mess up.

WHAT'S THE STORY YOU TELL YOURSELF?

During my training in ThetaHealing (energy and mindset work), I had a major revelation.

I realized that I had this savior complex.

I thought my worth came from being the one to "save others" and fix their problems. I felt responsible for other people's pain and their healing, so much so that I just felt the need to help them at the cost of my own mental health.

I thought that I was being "nice" by sacrificing myself, which then made me feel worthy in turn.

But I was so wrong.

Being nice doesn't mean neglecting yourself or sacrificing your own needs.

It doesn't mean running yourself into the ground for the sake of others, to the point that your physical body can't function anymore.

It doesn't mean giving up your health for something outside of yourself, all for the chase of being seen as "worthy" by someone else.

HOW TO BREAK FREE

1. **Screw perfectionism!**

    We have this ridiculous notion that if we were truly talented and good enough, we would never make mistakes, know everything, never doubt ourselves, never need any support or help, and be successful at everything we do.

    But that's just not true.

    In a recent entrepreneur event hosted in Sharjah, UAE, the CEO and million Steven (host of the podcast Diary of the CEO) spoke about how Richard Branson, the British billionaire, entrepreneur, and famously known as the founder of the Virgin Group, told Steven that he was dyslexic. He openly admitted that he's not good at everything, but he's still incredibly successful.

    In an interview with The Times, Richard Branson says that "Dyslexia is my superpower." He's convinced that his dyslexia was the reason he took risks.

    Every single successful person has their own challenges, but what puts them at their place at the top is that they don't allow those challenges or the need for perfection to ruin their success.

So, repeat after me, perfectionists:

"Always trying to be perfect at what I do is not neither healthy for me nor is it possible. I recognize that I am no longer avoiding things due to fear of failure as I am starting to see mistakes and setbacks as a learning experience that will redirect me to something better."

Put this affirmation on your bathroom or bedroom mirror. Wherever you'll see it often.

Your worthiness has nothing to do with "how perfect you are". You are worthy of creating a beautiful life and becoming everything you want to be, imperfections and all.

And who knows, those very imperfections that you hate so much might just be what sets you apart and propels you forward.

2. **Your current place is not your final destination.**

Are you stuck in a place in your life that you absolutely hate? A place that feels miles away from where you truly want to be?

If yes, then please take a deep breath. You're not alone, I promise you. No matter how deep you think you've fallen, whether you've hit rock bottom, lost all your money, failed at school, had a relapse, living in your parents' or grandparents' basement, crashing on a friend's couch, got fired, quit your job, left a toxic relationship, currently still in a toxic relationship, moved abroad, are scared, anxious, depressed, heartbroken, lost, going through health or mental challenges, I see you. I really do.

And I just want to remind you that where you are right now is not where you're going to stay… unless you let it be.

You have the power to change your story whenever you want. Don't sit around waiting for your fairy tale to magically happen. You have to take control and write your own story.

You know, most successful people didn't start in the best positions either.

JK Rowling was rejected by publishers 12 times before she published "Harry Potter".

Dr Phil was even homeless at one point.

Halle Berry lived in a homeless shelter.

Jim Carrey lived in a van and on his sister's lawn.

Millionaire Chris Gardner, the guy who inspired the movie "The Pursuit of Happyness", was homeless with a young son.

Steve Harvey, the actor and TV personality, was also homeless when he started out as a comedian.

Suze Orman, the Emmy-winning financial advisor and New York Times bestselling author, lived out of her van too.

Yusra Madini, a Syrian refugee who became a successful Olympic swimmer, quite literally swam for her life during the civil war in Syria. When things got really intense, she had to flee the country with her sister, and swimming was their ticket to safety.

And remember Richard Branson, the British billionaire and founder of the Virgin Group? He dropped out of school at 15!

Then we have Ursula Burns, a successful businesswoman and head of a Fortune 500 company. She grew up in a rough housing project in Manhattan, an area that was known for its gangs. Her mum worked 2 jobs just so Ursula could go to school.

Indra Nooyi went from a humble family in India to becoming the CEO and Chairwoman of PepsiCo. She was the first woman of color and the first immigrant to head a Fortune 500 company.

Hal Elrod, the successful bestselling author of Miracle Morning, was clinically dead for six minutes and in a coma for six days. He even broke 11 bones! Doctors told him that he may never walk again, but guess what? He didn't allow his diagnosis to be his death sentence.

Tim Ferris, an American entrepreneur, investor, and the host of the famous Tim Ferris show, also went through some seriously tough times. He tried to commit suicide and was sexually abused from a young age. But he didn't let any of that define him and rose above it all.

Dr Joe Dispenza was hit by a truck, broke six vertebrae in his spine, and was told he would never walk again. What did he do? Well, he became a New York Times bestselling author and researcher.

So, even if you're not dealing with extreme circumstances like these people, take a look around. Your parents, for example. Did they have to work 5 times harder to give you the life you have? Maybe they were immigrants, single parents, or struggled with health and financial issues. They had to overcome all of that to provide for you.

Let these stories, and the ones in your own life, remind you that nothing is impossible.

Because hey, most successful authors, musicians, coaches, entrepreneurs, lawyers, business owners, all started from zero. Some even ran on minus.

Do you think any of these people would be where they are now if they believed that where they were was their final destination? No! They took charge and created a whole new life for themselves.

And their families and generations to come.

Now, I'm not saying it's going to be a walk in the park. Writing a new life script is the hardest thing anyone can do. But trust me, it's the best decision you will ever make. And guess what? You don't need superpowers or anything like that. Anyone can do it.

I mean, how many more success stories do you need to hear to realize that there's still hope, no matter where you are right now? So, take that frustration and turn it into massive action, just like Tony Robbins says.

Make those changes you know you need to make.

3. **Don't let the past anchor you.**

So many of us carry around the voices of our parents or toxic relationships, telling us that we're not worthy. We allow these voices to be louder than the truth of our own worth.

I've learned that in order to become the person you want to be, you have to let go of who you were. You have to let go of those echoes from the past.

Just because your ex or toxic friend told you that you're unworthy, or your parents made you feel undervalued, doesn't mean that's who you are now.

You are worthy. Feeling loved and valued is your birthright.

Don't let anyone else tell you otherwise.

"People decide what you're like before they even get to know you. They think they know all about you. Except, you're never who they think you are. – Celeste Ng, Everything I Never Told You

CHAPTER 8

LIE #8: YOUR VALUE AS A HUMAN IS BASED ON YOUR BODY SIZE

I used to be scared of food. Terrified that eating would make me gain weight. I carried this fear from as early as I could remember and, for over 17 years, I struggled with my relationship with my body and food.

It started when I was just 8 years old. The classic story. I was that chubby kid with the chubbiest cheeks (which might sound cute and all, but it didn't feel like it at the time) and I always felt like I didn't "fit in". I would compare myself to other girls every single day, especially my older (and slimmer) sister. Whenever my mum dressed us in the same outfit, I would wonder why I didn't look as pretty as she did.

I mean, yes, we may have looked cute and picturesque on the outside as sisters but internally, I hated everything about it. I used to think that wearing the same dress would make everyone else compare us even more too, by noticing the weight difference between us and seeing how each dress would sit on me compared to my sister.

It was the beginning of my self-loathing and low self-esteem.

Being different in appearance and culture at my primary school didn't help either. I would obsessively think about how "chubby" or "fat" I was. I stood out with my olive skin, dark brown bob haircut with an uneven full fringe, thick messy eyebrows, and a unique nose. I spoke a different language at home and ate different foods. I did not fit in with all the other kids.

I mean, I was an Egyptian Muslim girl in a Catholic primary school just trying to find her way.

My earliest memories of that time were me being called "chubby" and "fat" and being made fun of for my weight. I remember being told that I should "stop eating because I'm already a big round ball and wouldn't fit through the door." I was always picked last for sports and games. It's a story many people who have been bullied can relate to.

And if you're one of those who've been bullied growing up, you'd know how every single one of these words stick.

Those apparent ethnic physical differences were one thing, but the constant teasing about my weight during school years was definitely the main factor that threw me into a toxic cycle of hating my body and food. It lasted for 17 years.

Yes, you read that right, 17 whole years.

It's only in the past year, at 27 years old, that I've started to heal and become aware of it all.

I used to believe that losing weight would bring me happiness. But when I did lose weight, I felt worse than ever. The happiness and the dream life did not follow. I was constantly hungry, tired, and sick.

Why? Well, because I did it the unhealthy way. I starved myself, restricted certain foods, and beat myself up for any indulgence. I eliminated the majority of foods from my diet, labeled them black or white, and over-exercised. It became a dangerous cycle of negative thoughts and behaviors when it came to eating and my relationship with my body.

I became so weak that I had chronic pain and severe hormonal issues. All of this just to chase the illusion that being "slim" would make me feel "worthy".

It's all a big lie.

Why do we risk our lives and mental health for a fake pot of gold called thinness? Some people even lose their lives in pursuit of it. Is it really worth it?

(I ask myself this too, as someone who fell into that trap for 17 years and is only just starting to climb out.)

WHY?

WHY do so many of us have toxic relationships with food and our bodies, especially as women? Just why?

Well, I believe it's because of diet culture. Everywhere you look, there's a woman complaining about her body or feeling guilty for eating certain foods.

Diet culture has made us afraid of food.

It has made us guilt and shame ourselves for enjoying it.

It's very sneaky too. It disguises itself as a "lifestyle" rather than a diet, tricking us into thinking that it's connected to health and wellness. But deep down, it's still the same old restrictive mindset. Everyone is now aware that diets don't actually work but we have yet to outgrow this model. Majority of the time, whatever "lifestyle" they are trying to sell you is still a diet.

Diets plant the seeds for eating disorders and a general disordered relationship with food and our bodies. Why? Because diets require elimination, black and white thinking, and restriction.

And FYI, eating disorders also operate on these same internalized diet culture beliefs.

Now, I'm not a nutritionist or anything, but it's pretty funny (well, not really) how starving yourself or cutting out certain foods actually makes your body hold onto fat more. I mean, it actually has the opposite effect to what people generally expect.

Why does that happen? Because your body thinks there's a shortage of food and it needs to protect itself in order to survive.

So, how can we tell the difference between real lifestyle changes and diets pretending to be lifestyles? Well, if a "diet" makes you feel guilty or ashamed about what you eat, then it's probably not a lifestyle change.

If it makes you second guess and obsess over every little thing you put in your mouth, then it's definitely not a lifestyle change.

If it doesn't encourage you to eat until you're satisfied, then it's definitely a diet.

And if a diet promotes fat phobia or food phobia in any way, then sorry (not sorry), but it's definitely a DIET.

Real lifestyle changes prioritize your mental and physical well-being above all else. They don't tie your self-worth to your body size. There's no fear of being "fat" or fear of food involved, because that's not how we're meant to live as strong individuals.

I believe diet culture was created to disempower women, making them so obsessed with their weight and appearance that they don't have the mental capacity to realize their true feminine power. Because if women woke up to their dormant power, the world would have to change.

Now, many people ask me how I learned to love my body after the sheer self-loathing and hatred I used to have with it – to the point where I would avoid mirrors just so I wouldn't have to see myself.

Let me tell you, as a child and up until my late teenage years, I had such a toxic and unhealthy relationship with my body that I would hit my "chubby" stomach so hard that I sometimes bruised my ribs.

My journey to loving my body started when I realized how miraculous it is and how much it does for me without me even realizing. This realization came to me when I hit rock bottom. They say "you don't realize what you have until it's gone," and that's especially true for your health.

After being hospitalized multiple times when I hit my rock bottom during which I was not able to sleep, drive or even properly walk without getting dizzy serves as a constant reminder for me now that every breath, sight, touch, and sound is a gift I am grateful for.

It's the same when it comes to a loved one's health. After a few too many health scares from both of my parents, I've come to realize what a blessing it is for them to simply just be OK.

We often take our health for granted.

So now, thanks to nourishing myself in a healthy way and avoiding society's diet culture trap, I can now think creatively, enjoy life, and appreciate the miracles my body can do.

What a miracle it is that my arms can carry bags of food, clap, write, draw, and cook. That they can hug my parents, squeeze my little nephew whenever I see him.

What a miracle it is to move my body in ways I didn't even know was possible through practices like Yoga and Pilates.

Treating your body with the awe and the respect it deserves is so important. Deepak Chopra (who was previously a traditional medical doctor) calls our bodies a pharmacy. A pharmacy that provides us with everything we need, with the perfect dose and instructions within us.

The body knows exactly how to heal itself. It's much smarter than we give it credit for. I mean before modern medicine, how did older tribes and communities heal illness, disease and health challenges? They believed in the power of nature and the body.

Our body isn't just a representation of our body size or weight or what society told us. Our body is a representation of the miracle of life.

I want to inspire every woman to choose how she wants to look and show up, instead of blindly following society's expectations.

The beauty industry, worth billions of dollars, has influenced us for years, making us feel insecure and pushing us to look a certain way. It scams women, using makeup and dressing, and wastes no time in trying to make a profit by preying on their insecurities.

Movies and TV shows also play a role, often featuring the "picture perfect girl next door" as the popular one who obviously gets everything she wants, while her "chubbier, less attractive" best friend is ignored who no one wants to date and who is the "dork" that no one wants to be.

Let's be honest here. I don't think any of us really wanted to be that friend. But you know what? I was, and I did everything I possibly could to NOT BE HER.

Working as a school counselor opened my eyes to the dangerous effects of comparing ourselves to our friends, especially at a young age. It can lead to some seriously harmful behaviors like hating our own bodies, binging and purging, starving ourselves, popping diet pills, using laxatives, or even turning to smoking to suppress our appetite.

These toxic thought patterns can even sneak up on me from time to time.

Just a few months ago, I went shopping with my mum and ended up in the dressing room, crying my eyes out and feeling completely hopeless. Why? Because my pants size had gone up due to gaining some HEALTHY weight back.

I had to remind myself of how far I've come on this journey.

There are days when you just don't feel your best, or those old insecurities try to creep back in, but you can't let them drag you down completely. You're so much stronger than that.

Let me share this quote from a 63-year-old actress Emma Thompson, who really hits the nail on the head:

"Because we're not used to seeing untreated bodies on the screen, we're only used to seeing bodies that have been trained. Most women can't stand in front of a mirror and not do anything. Many of us might turn to the side, pull the stomach in, they'll do something. Most women won't be able to just stand there. But

that's the problem isn't it? That women have been brainwashed all our lives to hate our bodies, that's the fact of it. Everything that surrounds us reminds us of how imperfect we are and everything is wrong with us. Everything is wrong and you need to look like this. You try standing in front of a mirror, take your clothes off and don't move, just accept it and don't judge it. It's the hardest thing I ever had to do."

I was recently listening to a podcast about Marilyn Monroe's life. We all know who she was. The epitome of femininity and beauty. Everyone was so obsessed with her. Men wanted her, women wanted to be her. But what most people don't know is that she grew up in foster homes because her mum struggled with severe mental health issues (possibly schizophrenia).

Marilyn had her own extreme insecurities and was always seeking love (some claim that was for her to finally feel wanted and worthy). She also battled depression, anxiety, and crippling stage fright whenever she acted in her moves.

Another example is Princess Diana, who was known to have struggled with an eating disorder.

These stories serve as a reminder that many women may appear a certain way on the outside but feel completely different on the inside.

But let me tell you something: **no matter what, we are more powerful, beautiful, and worthy beyond our wildest imaginations.**

"Our deepest fear is not that we are inadequate. Our deepest fear is that we are powerful beyond measure. It is our light, not our darkness that most frightens us." – Marianne Williamson

There's a really great video that I found on social media one day, where children were asked "if they could change one thing about their body, what would it be?"

And their answers made me cry.

Here are some examples of their answers:

"I would add a mermaid tail."

"I would have big shark teeth so I can eat more."

"I would have wings."

"I would be able to teleport."

"Nothing. I would change nothing about my body."

See how their answers are rooted in imagination, fun, and creativity? Rather than insecurity, self-hate, and fear?

If someone asked you this question now, how would you answer?

My answers a few years ago would be an endless list of everything I hated about myself.

But now… you know what? I would change nothing.

Well, actually, to be completely honest with you, maybe I wouldn't mind adding some sparkly fairy wings. I mean, imagine how much we would be able to save on flights!

HOW TO BREAK FREE

1. **Stop with all the shame.**

    First things first, stop beating yourself up over your body, self-image, or relationship with food. There's absolutely nothing "wrong" with you.

    Keeping it all bottled up only fuels the shame and unhealthy behaviors. So, please find someone you trust and let it out.

2. **Remember that it's YOUR plate.**

    Don't let other people's opinions mess with your eating habits. I mean, everyone and their grandma have something to say about what you "should" be eating. But guess what? It's your stomach, not theirs.

I don't care if their keto, paleo, vegan, low carb, no sugar, no oil, raw foods diet, or intermittent fasting did wonders for them – you do what's best for YOU. It's on your plate, NOT theirs.

And honestly, with all the conflicting information out there today, it's easy to get overwhelmed. There are videos out there telling you how anything you eat is "wrong", even if it's healthy. I mean, there are even videos claiming that drinking water is deadly. Come on now.

3. Don't fall into the diet cult.

Remember when we talked about the difference between a diet and a lifestyle? Well, here's your reminder: if a certain eating plan makes you feel worse, guilty, or obsessed, it's time to hit the brakes. Feeling shame or having your mental health affected in any way means you need to stop IMMEDIATELY.

Some people are so fanatical about their diets that they try to drag everyone else into it too. But your nutritional needs are unique to you. There's no one size fits all plan.

So, experiment, listen to your body, and find what works for you.

4. **You still need to eat.**

   No matter how much you ate yesterday, your body still needs nourishment today.

   After a day of overeating or binging, the last thing you should do is restrict yourself. Your body requires fuel and sustenance.

   Trust me on this, I've been caught in this vicious cycle for over 15 years, and it only makes things worse. Much, much worse.

   So please, listen to your body and give it the sustenance it deserves.

5. **Be an amateur.**

   "That's all any of us are: amateurs. We don't live long enough to be anything else." – Charlie Chaplin

   We're all amateurs in life. We're not born with all the answers or skills. Traditional schooling doesn't give us the space or patience to be amateurs as we are. It has made us believe that we're either naturally talented or we just don't have a chance.

But, as we discussed in chapter 3 about how ridiculously limited traditional schooling is, let's not let that nonsense define our lives.

You have the potential to excel at anything you set your mind to. It's not about being an "expert" or feeling pressured to be one. Just be good or great, whatever works for you.

So, if you're new to the world of healthy eating, cooking at home, stretching or working out, don't get discouraged when it takes some time to find your feet. I remember feeling so awkward and self-conscious when I first started Pilates and Yoga. I was like, WHAT IS THIS! I mean, I couldn't keep up for the life of me.

I was that girl in the corner who was constantly falling over and looking around in awe at the other girls who seemed to be able to twist and turn with ease, like they were made of rubber. Did they even have bones? Were they human or just human-sized spaghettis? And how were they even SMILING during this torture session?

It made me feel even more insecure when I noticed that most of these girls looked like they stepped right out of an Instagram feed or yoga magazine. They didn't even need to work out! Their outfits matched perfectly, while there I was in my oversized t-shirt, struggling to catch my breath and my hair stuck on my sweaty face.

But despite all the self-doubt, I pushed through. I completed one class, then another, and another. I reminded myself that every girl in that class was once a beginner, an amateur, just like me (unless they all came out of the womb doing headstands).

"Amateurs know that contributing something is better than contributing nothing.

Amateurs might lack formal training, but they're all lifelong learners, and they make a point of learning in the open, so that others can learn from their failures and successes.

The world is changing at such a rapid rate that it's turning us all into amateurs. Even for professionals, the best way to flourish is to retain an amateur's spirit and embrace uncertainty and the unknown." – Austin Kleon, Show Your Work!

So, don't be afraid to take the necessary steps to fall back in love with yourself and your body. For me, it was yoga and Pilates. Explore different paths and find what works for you.

Being an amateur is an exciting journey because the only way to go is UP. Stay consistent, stay passionate, and success will follow.

6. **Be an outlier.**

Being liked and accepted is a natural instinct stemming from our ancestors' need for survival.

Back in the days when tribes provided shelter, water, and food, being part of a tribe was crucial. I mean, think about it, our ancestors could only survive IF they were a part of some tribe – otherwise, they would be thrown out, left to fend for themselves out in the wilderness.

However, in today's world, this need to "fit in" is no longer a matter of life or death. Sure, it has been passed down to us, but we no longer live in tribes. We no longer live in a time where being part of a group is crucial to our survival. I mean, come on, if you don't fit into the popular group in high school, does that mean you will just simply DIE? Of course not!

It's time to break free from the pressure of conforming to societal norms and embrace our authentic selves. We don't need to play the popularity game or seek acceptance from just anyone to feel "safe".

Be the outlier, the one who stands out from the masses and follows their own path.

7. Redefine nice.

Your worth should never be determined by how much others accept you. Being nice should NEVER come at the expense of your mental and physical well-being.

Prioritize your own self-care and don't sacrifice your own happiness for the sake of pleasing others.

8. Let go of the "more" mentality.

"If you live for having it all, what you have is never enough." – Vicki Robin

Let's be real. No matter where you are in your journey, there will always be more to learn. However, we often underestimate how much we've already accomplished. Everything that you have learned to this point is invaluable, and it's time to start treating it as such.

Take a moment to reflect on how far you've come in the past five years and acknowledge your progress. You've grown and learned so much.

Whenever you face new challenges and feel like you're not fully equipped, remember that you are capable of handling them. As a beautiful saying (that I love to live by) goes, "God does not give you more than you can handle."

CHAPTER 9

LIE #9: WHEN YOU FIND LOVE, EVERYTHING WILL BE PERFECT

Disney taught us this. Fairy tales taught us this. Movies taught us this.

We've been conditioned to believe that when we find our soulmate or partner, everything will be perfect.

They'll complete you, heal you, and be your other half or "better half".

They'll be the sole source of your happiness and all your problems will magically disappear.

But let's get real for a second. Meeting your person can be amazing and make you feel on top of the world. I mean, I had that feeling when I met my husband. As cliché as it sounds, I just knew he was the one without a doubt. And he truly is the best thing that has ever happened to me. Every day, I wake up grateful for him, to have him.

But here's the thing, that doesn't mean that all my problems vanished or that I was instantly "healed" when we met or got married.

Being in a conscious, healthy relationship is the biggest form of spiritual work.

Why? Because it helps you become more aware of yourself and of areas that need inner healing. It's like a gateway to personal growth and becoming the best version of yourself.

But let me tell you, it's not easy.

Growing, being vulnerable, and communicating honestly are all tough – and those are required in real relationships.

We are creatures of habit, resistant to change, so we find it hard to move on and grow. Our survival instincts don't like it.

Raw vulnerability is hard too.

And real, honest communication is even harder.

Being in a relationship has forced me to confront my insecurities, past traumas, fears, and inner demons instead of hiding them or resorting to unhealthy coping mechanisms.

So, what I'm trying to say here is, a relationship or friendship can provide support while you gather your broken pieces and start your healing journey. They can stand by you, cheer you on, listen to you, and be there for you when you need them. But ultimately, it's your responsibility to heal, find happiness, and make different decisions. You're the one doing the inner work, not them.

No relationship will ever "complete" or "fix" you because guess what? You were never broken in the first place. You never needed fixing. So, let's stop with this "other half" nonsense, OK? You're already 100% on your own, and your partner is too. Together, you can be 200% and beyond.

The growth and potential in a relationship, for both of you, are limitless. So, please, don't rush into finding a soulmate or getting married just because you think they'll heal or complete you. This self-created urgency is, I believe, why many women settle for unfulfilling relationships.

And hey, I'm not talking about those who discover the toxic traits AFTER marriage or their partners hid them well. I mean those women who know their partner has red flags and treats them poorly, yet marry them out of desperation, "old age", family pressure, societal pressure, or other external factors. They end up settling for way less than they deserve – a person who gives them the bare minimum, or even less!

But trust me on this. There's no deadline or "right time" to get married. It's all just a social construct that keeps changing. Back in the day, women were expected to get married at ridiculously young ages. I mean, in the 1950s, the average age to get married in America was 20!

But times have changed, and now we question those standards. In 2023, the average age rose to 28 and keeps increasing every year.

It was a long time ago when it was even normal for women to get married by the age of 14 or 15. But things were VERY different back then. I mean, women needed to get married so they could be taken care of financially as they were not allowed to work and did not have other rights as well. My own great grandmother got married at the age of 12, and my grandmother was married at 16. It was normal back then, especially in Egypt. Now, of course, it's unheard of.

It's frustrating how normal it is to ask women of a certain age why they're not married or found a partner yet. We've already talked about how rushing things only attracts the wrong person and pushes away the right one. Why? Because of ENERGY.

The energetic state that you get into is rooted in desperation and scarcity.

I mean, if you're desperate and operating from a scarcity mindset, would anyone be attracted to that?

So, when you're in a desperate and lower vibrational energy state instead of a confident and positive one, you end up attracting people who are in the same negative mindset or, even worse, toxic individuals who feed off your energy and bring you down ever more.

It's the Law of Attraction 101 – like attracts like.

So, if you want to attract a partner who is truly amazing and on the same wavelength as you, you need to be the best version of yourself as well. That means focusing on improving areas of your life, whether it be your physical health, finances, personal development, or career.

Start by joining a fitness class once a week, managing your budget, reading, pursuing hobbies that you've always wanted to do, attending workshops or networking events, or even traveling. You have endless options.

Now, here's a harsh truth: if you're unhappy while single, chances are you'll still be unhappy when you're in a relationship. Because guess what?

Wherever you go, THERE YOU ARE.

So, being in a relationship won't magically fix your problems or suddenly make you a positive person. It's on you to find that inner happiness and take responsibility for your own well-being. And when you start loving yourself again, finding joy in your own life, and stop desperately searching for someone to complete you, that's when your perfect match somehow shows up. It happened to me, and it has happened to many others who have found their soulmates.

They found them when they STOPPED searching.

It's amazing what can happen when you let go and surrender to the universe's timing.

Forget about society's expectations and opinions. You should live life on your own terms and at your own pace. Just think about how many people you know who have wasted years of their lives because they made decisions based on what others expected of them.

How many of them ended up in loveless marriages or pursued careers they despised just to please someone?

How many of them studied a subject they hated or stayed in soul-draining jobs because society told them that is what "success" is?

How many of them are in debt due to the grand wedding they had? (and yet, everyone STILL complained about the food.)

It's time to break free from this pressure and live authentically.

And here's a little fun fact: according to recent research done by the company Lowell in the UK, it was found that two thirds (that's 66%) of British people get into debt due to their wedding days! And that's just in the UK, which isn't culturally into "grand" weddings if we compare it to Arab or Asian weddings.

Many incredible women I personally know were pressured to do the whole "grand wedding" and are still recovering from it financially years later.

I mean, don't get me wrong, I'm not against weddings. They can be magical and unforgettable experiences if that's what you truly want. But nowadays, weddings have become an opportunity for consumerism to thrive.

Just look at the prices skyrocket when the word "bride" or "bridal package" is mentioned.

We've allowed society to dictate how we spend our money and turned weddings into a competition of who can have the biggest and most extravagant event. We've normalized couples and parents spending their entire life savings or going into debt just for a wedding day.

I've come to learn that the majority of our decisions are done out of fear.

I mean, if you don't have a big wedding… what will people say?

Comparing ourselves with others and their "big weddings" should never take away what is meant to be a beautiful and magical day instead. When I used to visit Egypt during the summers to see my extended family and grandmother, I remember this comparison of family members' weddings and how, because one cousin did a big 600-person wedding WITH a famous singer invited, the other cousin must also do the same, if not more.

It was ridiculous.

It's time to break free from this fear-based decision making.

I don't need to be the one to tell you that having a big wedding does not equal a happy marriage. But if you're someone who does want to go for a grand wedding then, by all means, you do you.

However, in this chapter, I'm talking to those individuals who don't want the stress and financial burden that comes with a big wedding, yet STILL do it due to societal, cultural, or family pressure pushing them into it.

YOU HAVE TO SETTLE

I know a girl who is stuck in a relationship with a guy who's always checking out other girls, is super controlling and selfish. But she's still with him. Why?

Well, because she has convinced herself that this is just what relationships are like. And when someone asked her why she puts up with it, she said it's because all her friends have relationships that are exactly the same.

Can you believe that?

This is because the reality that she surrounds herself is filled with guys like that. Men who are disrespectful are "normal" in her eyes. But remember when we spoke in previously chapters how we have a limited view of reality? This is why it's so important to be able to see beyond your limited view of what is "normal" and what others around you are doing.

Instead, check in with yourself. Does this feel right? Intuitively you know the answer, despite what others have told you.

We have this deep need to be accepted by society, which goes way back to our caveman days. Back then, being part of a tribe meant survival. If you were cast out or considered too "different" from them, you were basically left to die alone with no food, water, or shelter. So naturally, we learned to do whatever it takes to be part of the "tribe" – whether that's changing who we are or going against our own values.

Today, most of us still live the same way. Just swap this word "tribe" for "friendship," "group," "clique," "gang," or "community". We are willing to go against our own values and lose our authentic selves just to be accepted. In schools, if you didn't have friends, you were vulnerable or maybe even cased out or chosen last in games.

But here's the thing they didn't teach us: we actually have the power to choose our own "tribe". It's something I wish I knew earlier. You, yes, YOU get to choose your own place.

The society or group that we're born into doesn't define us or determine our final destination. We can change, grow, and find people who truly align with our mindset and values. And thanks to technology, connecting with like-minded individuals from all over the world is easier than ever. Which takes me to the final part of this chapter…

"You have to settle – you won't find what you're looking for." That's another lie.

How can you expect to attract a partner, friends, or life that's a 10, when you're currently at a 3?

HOW TO BREAK FREE

1. **Challenge what is "normal" and "accepted" by society.**

    You can get married at 40 or later.

    You can choose not to get married at all.

    You can study art, dance, theater, and other arts if you want.

    You can switch careers at any age.

    You can choose not to study in a university.

    You can reject a job you hate.

    Don't let fear hold you back from making decisions that really align with who you are and what you want. Don't let the fear of being judged by society, your parents, or your community lead you to making the decisions that aren't actually yours.

    You, and only you, make the rules.

No one else can dictate the course of your life or the decisions that you make.

2. **Focus on bettering yourself.**

How can you expect to attract a 10/10 partner or an amazing life if you're at 4/10 and not putting in the effort to improve yourself?

Trust me, I found my soulmate and husband when I started working on myself and going through my own healing journey.

3. **Never settle.**

I can't stress this enough. If I could get one message across the whole world, to every single woman out there, I would tell them: "DON'T SETTLE. WHAT YOU WANT IS OUT THERE. AND YOU ARE WORTHY OF IT."

I had to emphasize this message because many people don't realize that they can have a happy and fulfilled relationship and job. You need to know that you deserve to have such a life. Don't let anyone tell you otherwise.

And if you already do believe this… no, it does NOT only happen to "lucky" people.

I was told for YEARS that I couldn't find the person I wanted and that I had to lower my standards. Many even told me that the most important thing for my future partner or have is a "good job" and that's it. Which is so wrong.

You're not going to be in a relationship with a CV, or marry a bunch of accomplishments. You're going to be in a relationship with a real, multifaceted individual.

Despite all the pressure and conditioning, I didn't settle. And guess what? I found my perfect match.

You don't have to settle for a mediocre relationship or marriage just because it's "normal" either. What you want is out there, and you are absolutely worthy of it.

So, forget about the idea that there's a limited supply of "good men and women". That's just another bunch of lies we've been fed.

Your parents, your culture, your community – their standards don't determine your own.

You have the power to create the life and relationship you truly desire.

4. **Practice love languages on yourself.**

I used to have a really messed up relationship with food and my body for over 15 years before I decided it was time for a change.

So, I started practicing the 5 Languages of Love by Gary Chapman to help me rebuild my relationship with myself. And let me tell you, I still do these things for myself every day.

First up, we have **Words of Affirmation:**

- Practice daily affirmations.
- Journal your accomplishments.
- Replace your inner critic with motivating words.
- Create daily gratitude lists.
- Add inspirational quotes everywhere in your room.

Acts of Service:

- Make your bed every day.
- Create a more organized and aesthetically pleasing environment at home.

- Give yourself a day off work.
- Do the things you've been putting off.

Receiving Gifts:

- Buy yourself flowers.
- Take yourself out to eat at your favorite restaurant.
- Invest in courses or classes for personal growth.
- Book an activity that's been on your bucket list.

Quality Time:

- Go for a walk.
- Prioritize sleep and exercise.
- Don't overschedule your day.
- Meditate and practice mindful breathing.
- Cook yourself a nourishing meal.

Physical Touch:

- Create a skincare routine that makes you feel great.
- Moisturize your skin with creams, lotions, or oils mindfully.

- Get some exercise and stretch your muscles.

- Soak in a nice hot bath with Epsom salts.

- Give yourself a manicure, pedicure, facial, or hair mask treatment.

CHAPTER 10

LIE #10: FEMININE ENERGY IS A WEAKNESS

One of my biggest "aha" moments was when I learned about masculine and feminine energy. Turns out, we all have BOTH of these energies inside us.

Both masculine and feminine energies are necessary to be embodied to feel like a complete person.

Our masculine energy kicks in when we're working toward goals and getting things done. It thrives with structures and rules in order to apply logic properly. Characteristics include:

- Present and focused.

- Desire to protect and build.

- Ability to think clearly.

- Problem solving.

- Disciplined.

- Stable and predictable.
- Goal oriented.
- Independent.
- Rational and logical thinking skills.
- Enjoys challenges.
- Linear thinking.
- A desire for appreciation and admiration.

On the other hand, feminine energy is more flowing and intuitive. It's not constrained by social norms as its guidance comes from the heart and the soul.

Now, contrary to traditional opinions, the feminine energy is not weak. It is powerful. Really powerful.

So, what are some feminine energy characteristics?

- Creativity and inspiration.
- Ground and has strong boundaries.
- Prioritizing feelings.
- Nurturing and soft.

- Thinks in circular motion.

- Intuitive and more attuned to internal processes.

- Ability to empathize.

- Ability to make judgments based on intuitive instinct.

- Great communication skills.

- Community and connection.

- Flows with life.

- Connection to nature.

Being in your feminine energy doesn't mean that you're weak. It's quite the opposite, actually. When you tap into your feminine energy, you're able to create worlds and dive into an infinite source of knowledge and creativity.

This then begs the most important question… **Why are so many of us out of touch with our feminine energy traits? And even shame feminine energy?** Why does society value masculine energy more?

Well, in western society, masculine energy is what is related to "success" because it's all about independence, discipline, logic, and rationale. But we've seemed to have forgotten about the power of feminine energy – community, connection, creativity, and intuition – that drive our societies and many businesses forward.

When we focus too much on one energy, we end up feeling imbalanced. We lose touch with ourselves and our intuition. When we overvalue masculinity, we spend 99% of our time "hustling" and not enough time resting, in nature, or tapping into our creative energy. We spend more time on our screens instead.

Isn't it crazy to think that so many women today suffer from burnout, overwhelm, exhaustion, and fatigue? This is because us women are overworking and not giving ourselves enough time to connect with our feminine energy.

THE TAKEAWAY

There's no such thing as "better" energy.

I'm not taking sides here. But let's face it, our world is all about rewarding masculine traits – so much so that we often overlook and even shame feminine energy and its characteristics.

But guess what? When we embrace both energies within ourselves, it's like a power combo that brings us incredible fulfillment and purpose.

We've been conditioned to believe that only one type of energy is superior, when in reality, it's the combination of both that can really elevate our lives.

I mean, think about it. When we tap into our masculine energy, we become goal-oriented, focused, and driven to achieve. We channel our inner go-getter and strive for success. On the other hand, embracing our feminine energy allows us to connect with our intuition, empathy, and nurturing qualities.

So, why limit ourselves to just one energy when we have the potential to experience the best of both worlds?

We no longer have to choose between being strong and sensitive, assertive and nurturing. We can be all of it.

It's time to ditch the idea that feminine energy is weak.

Celebrate and honor the unique qualities that both energies bring.

Having a balance of both energies, the masculine and the feminine, and knowing when to tap into each one plays a crucial role in making your life and level of happiness and success filled with greater purpose, ease, and flow.

HOW TO BREAK FREE

1. **Cultivate your feminine energy.**

   Cultivating and tapping into your feminine energy can help heal, restore, and inspire you.

   Here are a few ways to do that:

   - *Add meditation to your day.*

     Only a few minutes of meditation will allow you the gift of reconnection to your body and your breath.

     It also allows the intellectual mind to take a back seat while you create space for your intuitive, creative, and present self.

     Even simply spending a few seconds of your day to do some mindful breathing can help you tremendously. Don't ever underestimate the power of breath.

   - *Get creative.*

     You don't have to be an expert. Just go ahead and try out that painting or pottery class you've been wanting to. Or simply journal or draw. Or anything else that will get your creative juices flowing!

- *Move your body.*

Add some movement such as dance, stretching, yoga, or simply walking. Any movement that can create more fluidity in your body and mind.

- *Take some me-time.*

Spend some time with yourself just "being", not doing.

For example, you can take a bath, listen to some calming music, or mindfully sip on some herbal tea.

- *Connect with nature.*

When we go back to the basics such as spending time with nature, our minds and bodies are able to reconnect and re-attune themselves to the natural rhythm and flow of line.

Not to mention, it's calming as heck.

You can do this by going on a walk or a hike, or simply sitting in the midst of a park or a beach.

You can even add some plants or flowers in your home and office to help you appreciate the beauty and simplicity of nature.

- *Incorporate a FLOW day.*

I started to incorporate this every so often after listening to the book "The Surrender Experiment" by Michael Singer. And it's been a game-changer.

If you're able to take a day or even a few hours where you don't have anything planned, have a FLOW day. Just go with the flow, no plans, no schedules. Let your body and intuition guide you. Trust me, this will make your intuition grow stronger than ever.

- *Be more vulnerable.*

By letting go of our egos and sharing our truth and struggles with others, we open up a safe for others which is the foundation of community. A major element of being in your feminine energy: connection and community.

Just like the incredible author and expert of vulnerability, Brene Brown says, *"In order for*

> *connection to happen, we have to allow ourselves to be seen – really seen."*

2. **Accept compliments just like a man does. Don't downplay or dismiss them.**

   In Shonda Rhimes' inspiring book, Year of Yes, she recounts attending a women's event where no woman was able to ACCEPT a compliment.

   It's crazy to think that even in a room filled with powerful and successful women, they continuously waved off their accomplishments and success.

   Being in touch with your feminine energy doesn't mean playing small or staying silent. Instead, it means being so self-assured and confident in yourself that your inner radiance shines through.

3. **Reframe your mind.**

   Reframe the belief that success can only be achieved through masculine energy.

   Numerous stories and podcasts featuring female CEOs and successful business owners have shown that intuition and creativity can be powerful tools for making business decisions.

Even introverts and those embodying feminine qualities can become self-made millionaires.

Remember, success knows no gender or energy type.

4. **Establish boundaries.**

By setting strong boundaries, you are embracing your feminine energy.

Practice saying "no" when necessary and prioritize your own needs.

If someone has an issue with your boundaries, it may be a sign that they aren't the best fit as a friend or partner.

Remember, **not everyone needs access to you.**

(This belief doesn't make you selfish or rude; it simply means you value and prioritize your own worth and integrity.)

Here's a helpful hack that has worked for many, including myself:

HACK #1 – Create an Emotional Bill of Rights:

Write down your **non-negotiable rules** for yourself on a piece of paper or in your phone's Notes section. This document should be easily accessible and visible to you.

Here's an example:

1. I am entitled to respect.

2. Doing what makes ME happy doesn't require others' understanding.

3. I know that I am worthy regardless.

4. Being myself is a fundamental birthright.

5. I am entitled to saying NO when it doesn't serve me.

6. My family origin does not have to be the family I identify with.

7. I am responsible for my own beliefs and decisions.

8. Even loved ones do not have the right to overstep my boundaries.

Sign here:

Now, create your own Emotional Bill of Rights and remind yourself of it whenever needed.

Let's make a pact together, right here, right now. You will NOT neglect these rules that you have put on yourself. Please treat them as seriously as you would any laws or regulations and abide by them. This is crucial.

It's time to prioritize what's best for you, isn't it?

"You are not required to set yourself on fire to keep others warm." – Unknown.

5. Use affirmations properly.

Simple affirmations alone won't do the trick.

You must genuinely feel the emotions and sensations associated with them.

When it comes to using affirmations, it's not just about saying them repeatedly like a broken record. You need to really FEEL them in your bones.

If you're standing in front of the mirror, reciting your affirmations with a smile on your face, but deep down, you're not really feeling it. Well, that's not going to cut it.

To make affirmations really work, imagine yourself already living the life you desire. Let the excitement, joy, and confidence wash over you.

For example, if you're saying "I am confident and capable," you have to summon that feeling of confidence. Picture yourself standing tall, shoulders back, and your head held high. Feel the surge of confidence within you. Believe in yourself. That's how you use your affirmations properly.

So, the next time you're using those affirmations, don't just say them – own them.

As Neville Goddard says "feeling is THE secret!".

6. **Eliminate toxic positivity from your life.**

The notion of "just think positively" overlooks the importance of all emotions.

I mean, life isn't always happy or positive. Sometimes, we feel sad, tired, angry, and that's normal. In fact, it's more than just normal; it's NECESSARY.

Every emotion serves a purpose and acts as a messenger.

Ignoring and suppressing your emotions in the name of "positive thinking" can do more harm than good.

You don't need to have a fake smile on and pretend that everything is going well when it's not. Instead, let yourself feel all of the emotions, the good and the bad, and learn from them.

That's how you grow and find genuine happiness.

CHAPTER 11

LIE #11: YOU NEED MORE TO BE HAPPY

"It is not the man who has too little, but the man who craves more, that is poor." – Seneca

We're constantly bombarded with the idea that we need more to be happy. Whether it's societal pressure, our own inner desires, or through advertisements.

According to a Gaia article, we are constantly being shown advertisements every minute of every day. I mean, some estimates even say that the average person sees up to **10,000 ads** in a single day! That's insane!

The result of this? Majority of us developing the belief that our existing possessions and achievements are never enough.

We see this play out in the story of a woman who is a successful CEO with a thriving business and has everything she could ever want. Money, fancy cars, dream house, you name it. She has enough to help herself, her parents, and even her friends for a better quality of life.

But she still feels unfulfilled.

She believes she can't be happy yet. Why? Because she's convinced that true happiness lies in achieving some elusive, prestigious award for her company.

And you know what? It's not just her – many of us fall into the same trap, thinking that our happiness is contingent upon achieving a certain goal or possessing a specific thing.

I don't mean this about the award, but about how we believe that once we achieve something or get that one thing or find that person we've been dreaming about, then we'll finally be happy.

It's a mindset that will always keep us unsatisfied. Perpetually. Always reaching for the next milestone, the next thing that is supposed to finally, finally make us happy.

This idea of keeping up with the Joneses is also described in Rich Dad Poor Dad:

"As your cash flow grows, you can indulge in some luxuries. An important distinction is that rich people buy luxuries last, while the poor and middle class tend to buy luxuries first. The poor and the

middle class often buy luxury items like big houses, diamonds, furs, jewelry, or boats because they want to look rich. They look rich, but in reality they just get deeper in debt on credit. The old-money people, the long-term rich, build their asset column first. Then the income generated from the asset column buys their luxuries. The poor and middle class buy luxuries with their own sweat, blood, and children's inheritance."

Does anyone honestly believe that making more money, consuming more stuff, driving a bigger car, or bagging that fancy title will make them happier?

Take a moment to think about the last time you achieved something you had been longing for. Maybe it was getting a job promotion or buying a new car.

How long did that feeling of accomplishment and happiness last? Was it a week? A month? Maybe even just a few days?

For many of us, it was only temporary. Before we find ourselves, yet again, setting new goals and chasing after the next big thing.

Let's stop and ask ourselves something: **Am I chasing after something that can never truly satisfy me?**

You see, it's a never-ending cycle that leaves us constantly CHASING happiness instead of actually EXPERIENCING it.

It's so easy to get caught up in the societal expectations of success and wealth. It's "normal" to think that these external factors will bring us lasting happiness. But so many of us waste our time and energy on getting things that won't actually bring us happiness.

We forget that true happiness lies in the simple pleasures of life – spending time with loved ones, creating meaningful connections, learning something new and simply having fun.

So, maybe, just maybe, it's time to reconsider our priorities and focus on what truly matters. To appreciate and enjoy the moments and memories that make our hearts and our souls come alive.

In the documentary Chasing the Present, Russel Brand said: *"Fear and desire provoke action. They cause you to get out of the present. If you are continually being frightened, turn on your TV set, look at your own terror, death, cancer, war, famine and then desire that comes inundated with beautiful imagery. And it's very hard. It's hard. I feel like cultures got jump leads on my consciousness. It keeps sending signals that are not helpful. It's not a coincidence, is it? Consumerism and capitalism? That's where we've all got to. That's what we've all generated through our consciousness. That's what we are all participating in and enough of us seem to find it hard to go, I'm just coming off Facebook, I'm coming off Google, I'm not even going to own this phone no more. I'm not going to earn money. I'm just going to sit quietly by the river and breathe.*

And that's the thing. I'll see if anyone's called while I've been breathing."

HOW TO BREAK FREE

1. **Whatever you give your energy to is what wins.**

   Do you place your energy on what you lack?

   Are you focusing on the material possessions, achievements, or even personal qualities that you *don't* have?

   If so, you need to get out of this endless cycle of feeling inadequate.

   Now, what if you shifted your focus?

   What if, instead of dwelling on what you don't have, you start paying attention to what you already have?

   Start counting your blessings, big or small. Maybe you have a supportive group of friends, a loving partner, or even just a warm cup of coffee in the morning.

   This may sound simple, but shifting your perspective and your mindset can be incredibly powerful. When you redirect your energy toward gratitude and acknowledging the wealth and abundance already present in your life, you can break free from the chains of scarcity mindset and start experiencing fulfillment.

2. **Reflect on your motivations.**

Before buying something, take a moment to reflect on why you really want it.

We live in a world where we are constantly bombarded with messages telling us what we should buy, what we should wear, and what we should aspire to be. This pressure forces us to chase after things and experiences that might not align with our own values and desires.

I mean, we've all fallen prey to the persuasive whispers of consumerism at some point. But before you click that "buy now" button or reach for your wallet, stop. Pause for a moment and ask yourself: why do you really want that thing you're about to buy?

Is it because society tells you it's the best, or is it truly what's best for you?

Letting society dictate our choices is like surrendering our individuality. It's time to break free from the crowd and start thinking for ourselves.

Trust your own judgment, follow your own intuition, and make careful choices that align with your values.

Don't be a sheep. Be the shepherd of your own life.

3. **Redefine what happiness means to you.**

On the Tony Robbins program called Personal Power, he spoke about how, when people were asked about what happiness or success means to them, some said that waking up every day is what happiness is for them.

It's different for everyone, so figure out what truly brings you joy and keep that as your standard.

4. **Practice gratitude every day.**

Now, I don't want to bore you with the gratitude card, but seriously, practicing gratitude helps you appreciate what you already have instead of fixating on what's missing.

Every single day, you wake up alive.

We don't realize the beauty of what we have until it's gone. I know this is cliché to say, but it's true. Just think about how you don't fully appreciate your health until you have a blocked nose or a sore throat.

Something as simple as that makes you realize what a blessing it was to be able to sleep and breathe with ease, or how you used to swallow so comfortably without realizing.

The same goes for when you have a bad back, an ear infection, strained ankle of thumb. Simply having something not right with any body part makes you even more grateful for the miraculous body that you have.

It's always the little things that we often take for granted.

Everything that is inside our bodies is exactly the perfect size and flows in a perfect way. Nature is simple. Yet we make it completed.

Every morning, we wake up. Alive. Isn't that us being lucky enough?

5. **Be flexible.**

Now, I'm not just talking in a yoga way, but in your mindset too. I mean flexibility in your beliefs and opinions, as the majority of our subconscious beliefs are formed in the first 7 years of our lives.

Don't be so rigid in your beliefs because things are constantly changing and evolving. The atoms within us are constantly jumping up and down. We are constantly vibrating a certain energy (even if you like or believe it or not).

So, being rigid or fixated on one belief system is not going to serve you in any way. You must slowly start to become more open to change and evolution.

Just look at nature, it's always adapting.

6. **Stop stressing about your life purpose.**

There are so many programs out there promising to help you "find your purpose", but really, it's just another form of procrastination or even victim mindset, if you will.

I've overheard this so many times, in so many conversations, and even had people come to me for advice. They would be waiting for this insight or magical awakening to happen that will show them their purpose so they can finally "quit their job and live the life of their dreams".

Don't fall into that trap.

What to do instead?
Simply follow the joy and try things out. I've found that's the best way to really figure out who you are rather than overthinking your life purpose, just take action and DO THINGS.

Life is about learning what feels good and unlearning what no longer feels good or resonates with you.

Trial and error is the best way to move forward when you're stuck on finding your life purpose. Just try something out, if it doesn't feel right, then try something else. That's the exciting part of living this life- you don't need to have it all "figured out", you can just simply figure out the next step in front of you and that's it.

FINAL THOUGHTS

"The Matrix is a system, Neo. That system is our enemy. But when you're inside, you look around, what do you see? Businessmen, teachers, lawyers, carpenters. The very minds of the people we are trying to save. But until we do, these people are still a part of that system [...] You have to understand, most of these people are not ready to be unplugged. And many of them are so inured, so hopelessly dependent on the system, that they will fight to protect it." – Morpheus, The Matrix

We made it. We made it together. You made it through.

I hope this book has shifted your way of viewing the world and yourself in a limited way and instead showed you the potential that you can be.

Every single thing you do is like casting a vote for the kind of person you want to become.

And here you are, reading this whole book to the end, showing that you're already on your way to becoming the best version of yourself and living your dream life.

I genuinely have tears in my eyes. I'm so honored that you gave me and this book your time and attention.

Want to know the one thing I'd like for you to take away from this book?

That you owe it to yourself to live the life you truly desire.

Forget about what society expects or wants from you. Please. You deserve the freedom of choice. The emotional freedom.

Let go of everything you think you know.

I mean, I had to let go of who I think I am in order to become the person I was destined to be.

Most people don't realize how powerful they are. We're not just a bunch of matter or atoms. Trust me, it's not easy to break free. That's why so many people don't even try.

Not everyone wants to be free. Some are content living in their cozy little comfort zones.

But by picking up this book and absorbing this knowledge, it means you're craving a change in your life.

This book was a project meant to challenge all the beliefs you thought you already had figured out.

The main thing I want you to do after reading this book is that I want you to ask for more.

More out of life.

More out of yourself.

More out of the friends around you.

More out of your marriage.

More out of your own potential.

I want you to be excited about your life, not just settling for the same old routine or accepting mediocrity.

All the work we do on ourselves becomes a gift we can share with everyone else.

Please, keep going. You owe it to yourself.

You can recreate yourself and your life from any moment, no matter what happened in the past. Your past doesn't define who you are now.

Sure, society may cling to its false narratives, but you now have the tools to think independently, seek out your own truth, and rewrite the story. You can reclaim your freedom.

This book gave you the practical tools of how.

And there has never been a better time to choose yourself. Time to set your own standards and stick to them.

Gone are the days of waiting to be chosen by someone else, whether it's a company, a boss, a publisher (that's why I self-published), an agent, or a partner. You don't need external validation to feel accomplished, worthy, or loved.

Now is the time to live beyond your wildest dreams without waiting for someone else to give you the green light.

You were made for so much more, and you've waited long enough for that "permission" you thought you needed.

By reading this book, you now have the right tools, and wisdom to break free from the patterns and conditioning society has imposed on you.

Commit to yourself. Commit to overcoming negativity. Commit to living a happier life that aligns with who you truly are.

The world needs you to use your voice now more than ever. It's time to step into your power.

Even if your vision isn't understood by others… you've got this.

Welcome to your new self.

CONNECT WITH ME

Dear you, I'd like to say a huge thank you for choosing to read Lies That Shaped You. If you enjoyed and want to keep up to date with all the life-changing tips and weekly inspiration I share, simply sign up to my community using the below link by scrolling down to Join the Community!

https://www.inspirewithyas.com/

Your email address will never be shared and you can unsubscribe at any time.

FREEIBES:

To get a FREE Self-Care Planner, use the link below:

https://www.inspirewithyas.com/freeresources-1

To get a FREE Goal Setting Secrets eBook, use the link below:

https://www.inspirewithyas.com/goalsettingebook

I hope you loved reading this book and if you did, I would be truly so grateful if you could write a review. I'd love to hear what your thoughts, and it makes such a huge difference in helping others discover this book so they can start their journey of transformation too.

Also, I'd be honoured to hear from you directly! Send me an email at yas@inspirewithyas.com and I'll answer you!

You can also DM me

https://www.instagram.com/inspirewithyas/ (inspirewithyas)

Check out my website at https://www.inspirewithyas.com/

Thank you so much once again. Looking forward to hearing from YOU!

Yas

REFERENCES

Altucher, J. (2013). *Choose Yourself!* Createspace Independent Pub.

Altucher, J. (2021). *Skip the Line*. Harper Business.

Andrews, C. (2020, May 24). Discovering your 'emotional home". Medium. https://candrews.medium.com/discovering-your-emotional-home-373208be4347

Ben Lionel Scott. (2018, July 12). *YOUR VALUE - Powerful Motivational Speech* [Video]. YouTube. https://www.youtube.com/watch?v=yBrRpb8aLwk

Cain, S. (2013). *Quiet: The Power of Introverts in a World That Can't Stop Talking*. Crown.

Cannon, J. (2016, July 13). *We All Want to Fit In*. Psychology Today. https://www.psychologytoday.com/us/blog/brainstorm/201607/we-all-want-fit-in

Caprino, K. (2020, October 22). Impostor Syndrome Prevalence In Professional Women And How To Overcome It. *Forbes*. https://www.forbes.com/sites/kathycaprino/2020/10/22/impostor-syndrome-prevalence-in-professional-women-face-and-how-to-overcome-it/?sh=b5fa50c73cbd

Chapman, G. (2015). *The 5 Love Languages: The Secret to Love That Lasts*. Northfield Pub.

Chary, M. (2019, October 7). *We're All Born Creative Geniuses Until School Systems Stifle It*. Gaia. https://gaia.com/article/does-education-kill-creativity

Chen, X., & Li, S. (2023). Serial mediation of the relationship between impulsivity and suicidal ideation by depression and hopelessness in depressed patients. *BMC Public Health*, *23*(1). https://doi.org/10.1186/s12889-023-16378-0

DeMarco, M. J. (2021). *Unscripted - The Great Rat-Race Escape: From Wage Slavery to Wealth: How to Start a Purpose Driven Business and Win Financial Freedom for a Lifetime*. Viperion Publishing.

Grant, A. (2021). *Think Again: The Power of Knowing What You Don't Know*. Penguin.

Honda, K. (2019). *Happy money: The Japanese Art of Making Peace with Your Money*. Gallery Books.

Kiyosaki, R. T. (2017). *Rich Dad Poor Dad: What the Rich Teach Their Kids about Money That the Poor and Middle Class Do Not!*

Lee, S. Y., & Hong, J. (2019). *The Having: The Secret Art of Feeling and Growing Rich.* Harmony.

Parsons, H. (2022, April 12). *Corporations Are Testing Ways to Advertise to Us in Our Dreams.* Gaia. https://www.gaia.com/article/corporations-are-testing-ways-to-advertise-to-us-in-our-dreams

Rhimes, S. (2016). *Year of Yes: How to Dance It Out, Stand In the Sun and Be Your Own Person.* Simon and Schuster.

Scarlet, J. (2020, October 2). *I Am Not Good Enough: Managing Imposter Syndrome.* Psychology Today. https://www.psychologytoday.com/us/blog/the-real-superheroes/202010/i-am-not-good-enough-managing-imposter-syndrome

TEDx Talks. (2011, February 16). *TEDxTucson George Land The Failure Of Success* [Video]. YouTube. https://www.youtube.com/watch?v=ZfKMq-rYtnc

The True Cost of a Wedding | Lowell Financial. (n.d.). https://www.lowell.co.uk/about-us/lowells-blog/lifestyle/the-true-cost-of-a-wedding/

Tony, T. (2023, May 19). Why Do People Do What They Do? | 6 Human Needs. tonyrobbins.com.

https://www.tonyrobbins.com/mind-meaning/why-you-are-the-way-you-are/

Ware, B. (2012). *The Top Five Regrets of the Dying: A Life Transformed by the Dearly Departing.* Hay House Incorporated.

www.ingramcontent.com/pod-product-compliance
Lightning Source LLC
Chambersburg PA
CBHW030545080526
44585CB00012B/263